Eduard Zeller, Theodore Dwight Woolsey, Henry Clay Vedder

The end of Luke's Gospel and the beginning of the Acts:

Two studies

historian. Perhaps he designed to be more full when he should continue his narrative of the events subsequent to the departure of Christ from the presence of his disciples. This continuation, or second book, he may have already projected, and meanwhile Theophilus, an 'instructed' Christian, had already so much knowledge of the great facts of the life of Christ that a brief notice was all that was here demanded. The ascension pointed in two directions, — towards the life on earth thus glorified at its close, and towards the kingdom of heaven, begun by apostolic labors and by the presence of the Holy Spirit, for which Christ's going away was essential.

Very little difficulty has been found by most of the commentators in attempting to reconcile the two narratives. Thus, Euthymius Zigabenus, in commenting on Luke xxiv. 50, simply says: "He [Jesus] led them out not then, but on the fortieth day after the resurrection. For the evangelist passed over ($\pi\alpha\rho\acute{\epsilon}\delta\rho\alpha\mu\epsilon\nu$) the intermediate events." And it is enough to refer to Ellicott's lectures on the life of Christ as expressing the current modern opinion on this point.

Meyer, however, a careful, able, honest, and Christian scholar, — one who changed many of his opinions between the publication of the first editions of his commentaries and his death, — took quite another view of the relation between the end of Luke and the beginning of Acts — a view which he continued to take as long as he lived. There was a twofold tradition, he thought; one of them to the effect that Jesus ascended to heaven on the very day of the resurrection (Luke xxiv.; Mark xvi.); the other, that he remained on earth quite a number of days (Matt.; John), or, more definitely, forty days (Acts i.): "Luke in the Gospel followed the first tradition, but in the history of the apostles the second; which, therefore, he first became acquainted with after composing his Gospel, or, what is more probable, then first made his own."

We might say here that the first Gospel makes no mention at all of the ascension; and the same is true of the fourth,

BIBLIOTHECA SACRA.

ARTICLE I.

THE END OF LUKE'S GOSPEL AND THE BEGINNING OF THE ACTS. TWO STUDIES.

BY THEODORE D. WOOLSEY, D.D., LL.D., LATELY PRESIDENT OF YALE COLLEGE.

I.

AT the close of his Gospel, Luke, or whoever may be the author of the Gospel called by his name, subjoins immediately to the account of the risen Christ's visit to the eleven, on the evening of the resurrection day, the narrative of the ascension. In doing this he gives no notice to the reader that any interval of time passed between the two events longer than that between early morning and early evening. At the beginning of the second narrative, however, we find him declaring that the ascension took place forty days after the resurrection, and that there were repeated interviews between Jesus and the apostles in this period of time. If Luke had not written a second book, no other explanation (of the end of the Gospel) could have been admitted, save that he conceived of the ascension as taking place on the same day with the resurrection. But the first book has been almost uniformly interpreted by the second. There has been a general agreement that Luke threw together in a summary way, at the close of his first narrative, the last events which he had intended to include in it, without pointing out their distance from one another, — without that historical perspective, in short, which we should expect from a practised

Eduard Zeller, Theodore Dwight Woolsey, Henry Clay Vedder

The end of Luke's Gospel and the beginning of the Acts:
Two studies

ISBN/EAN: 9783337714185

Printed in Europe, USA, Canada, Australia, Japan

Cover: Foto ©ninafisch / pixelio.de

More available books at **www.hansebooks.com**

as far as direct historical statement is concerned, although the ascension is referred to more than once. And again, the end of Mark seems to be founded chiefly on Luke, and has in itself, we must believe, no independent authority. Now, as there is no evidence from any other source except the Gospel of Luke of an ascension in the evening of the day of the resurrection, the most that can be said is that Luke supposed when he wrote his Gospel that the ascension followed the resurrection by a few hours, but that afterwards, when he wrote the Acts, he discovered his mistake, or that he now believed and "made his own" what he had doubted before.

1. Our first inquiry will be: Can this be by any possibility admitted, if we admit also: (what Meyer decidedly admits) that the Gospel of Luke and the Acts belong to the same author, which may be held to be as well established by Zeller, Lekebusch, and others as the authorship of any books of the New Testament, unless some of Paul's Epistles be excepted? We also assume that the person called Luke, and spoken of in the Acts and in some of the Epistles as Paul's companion, was, as Meyer believes, the author of the two books mentioned. We further assume that the Gospel of Luke, as Meyer holds, was composed between the seventieth and the eightieth year of our era. This, however, is not necessary to our argument; for if we put it later, as the Tübingen school have tried to do, the probability of two traditions in respect to the time of the ascension becomes less and less.

This companion of Paul, whom we will call Luke, and who, as nearly everybody holds, in his narrative of events in the life of Paul where he uses the pronoun "we" borrows from no other person's journal, records his own companionship with the great apostle, first, in Acts xvi., then again in Acts xxvii. He goes with the apostle from Philippi on his last journey to Jerusalem, is with him at Caesarea, and went with him to Rome. He was with him when the Epistles to the Ephesians, Colossians, and Philemon were written, and only Luke was at his side when the second letter to Timothy (which I hold to be genuine) was penned, probably near the close of the apostle's life. Thus his attendance on the apostle must have included portions of the time between the years 52 and 62 A.D.; and if the letter to the Colossians belongs to a later period, his intimate acquaintance with the apostle must have begun before the First Epistle to the Corinthians was written, and have continued through several years afterwards. That in those years of close intimacy with Paul Luke had never heard of Christ's spending a number of days on earth after his resurrection, while yet the apostle taught the Corinthians the story of Christ in this shape, seems to be entirely incredible. For it is manifest that the presence of Christ among the twelve on the evening of the resurrection (1 Cor. xv. 5) was that recorded by Luke as then taking place; and the manifestation of Christ to the five hundred brethren, to James, and to all the apostles were all subsequent to this. How, then, could Luke fail to know of these events of such importance, which Paul knew of, and believed to have taken place after the resurrection evening? And how could Luke have failed to find accounts of these subsequent events in the narratives to which he refers in the prologue to his Gospel?

Considering, then, that the author of Luke's Gospel was one and the same person with the author of the Acts, that he was acquainted with the ascension when he wrote his Gospel, and must have known long before what Paul taught and received, in the many years of his familiar intercourse with the apostle, we can accept of no other explanation save that which looks on the end of chap. xxiv., probably from vs. 44 onward, as containing a summary of occurrences which, if historical exactness had been followed, were separated from the resurrection by a considerable interval of time.

2. We may draw from the narrative in Luke xxiv. 13–35 a subsidiary argument which makes it probable that Luke himself would have regarded the resurrection day as too short for including the ascension also. Here we are directly

concerned, not with the true state of the case, but with what would naturally be the impressions of the evangelist. The two disciples who went on that day to Emmaus, distant sixty stadia from Jerusalem, — or somewhat over seven English miles, — reached their destination at a time which is described in the words, "It is towards evening, and the day is far spent." The description of the time may be, we allow, incorrectly translated in the Authorized Version, and in the recently published revision which follows it. Ἑσπέρα, Luke's word for evening, like ὀψία, which is alone used by the other evangelists, has a meaning not exactly corresponding with our evening. Both words may include a part of the afternoon; and here πρός implies that ἑσπέρα was not yet reached. It was not the time denoted in the words *inumbrante vespera* of Tacitus (Hist. iii. 19), nor the δείλη ἑσπέρα of the Greeks, especially of the later writers (e.g. Appian, Hispan. § 114), *the later evening*, but an earlier part of the day. So while ὀψία in Matt. xxvii. 57 was considerably later than the ninth hour, it was in Matt. xiv. 15 early enough for the feeding of the multitude before nightfall. And yet in the same chapter it is used to denote a time not long before dark. And again, Luke, in ix. 12, uses the expression ἡ ἡμέρα ἤρξατο κλίνειν of a time early in the afternoon, after which the feeding of the five thousand took place. In the present case, it was late enough for the disciples to use the time as a reason why the stranger should stay with them, that is, to stay over night. Let us now suppose that the walk to Emmaus was commenced before midday, and required three hours nearly for its completion, as the interesting discourse would naturally make the progress somewhat slow, and that an hour or an hour and a half was consumed in the preparations for the meal and at the table. Thus the return of the disciples cannot begin till after three, or about half-past three o'clock. The return, — naturally at a quicker pace than that of the morning's walk, — might be accomplished by half-past five or a little later. Then the interview of the risen Lord, and the walk of a mile and three quarters to Bethany or Olivet, with the moments spent there until the ascension, would bring that event to a time quite too late, in the early part of April, to be fully discernible.

We do not, of course, mean to say that Luke made such calculations as these, and sifted with such minuteness every part of the history he was writing; but it is fair to argue that the compression of the events into the small space of time allowed to them ought to have been felt by the evangelist to be a crowding of events together which needed an explanation. Supposing the resurrection and the ascension to be myths, it would be easy to say that their relations to one another might be loosely adjusted; but if they were real events, no such difference of traditions as Meyer conceives of seems to be possible. And here we can appeal to John xx. 19–23, as containing the narrative of the same scene which Luke records (xxiv. 36), and as harmonizing with it substantially in regard to time. Only the time of day which we have assigned to the narrative in Luke, in order to give all fair weight to the possibility of the ascension taking place that same evening, would need to be brought down somewhat later in the evening.

3. We cannot reconcile the beginning of the Acts, on Meyer's view, with what one would expect from a conscientious man. If Luke had become convinced, after finishing his Gospel, that he had misstated a very important portion of the history of the Lord, he would have corrected the unintentional errors to which he had in his Gospel given currency. Instead of doing this, he refers to his Gospel in a way that puts a stamp of truth on it, and he seems unconscious of having said anything which he would now retract. The former narrative contained, he says, an account of the works and words of Jesus until the day when, after giving charges to his apostles, he was taken up into heaven; and then comes in a statement of what he did, and how long he stayed on the earth in a visible form. If verse 3 is intended as an alteration of his earlier book, it is inserted, we must believe, in an underhand way. He identifies the two accounts, and makes no explanations. He ought certainly to have

omitted, in that case, the words ἀκριβῶς and τὴν ἀσφάλειαν in his prologue, or have altered the end of the last chapter of his Gospel.

4. The considerations thus far advanced are confirmed by a peculiarity of Luke's composition, which appears chiefly in the Acts, where as a writer he was freer and more independent than in the structure of his Gospel. This peculiarity appears when he makes mention of the same event more than once, and may be described as the introduction of new particulars into the second or repeated narrative. The comparison of examples of this peculiarity will lead us to conclude that he did this purposely. The cause lay not in his forgetting particulars at the first mention of an occurrence and supplying the defect afterward, nor in following two manuscript authorities. It may be accounted for by his taste for lively narration, or by a desire to make mention of things at a place where they are especially needed. In support of this last explanation it may be alleged that in nearly all the cases the second mention (or the third, in one instance) is found in speeches coming directly from the principal person in the history. But we by no means assign any great weight to these suggestions, and are content to set forth the facts as they are.

Another less obvious peculiarity of Luke is a tendency to summarize, where many writers would have expressed something at greater length that they might avoid a certain incorrectness of expression. The most noticeable example of this is found in Acts xiii. 29: "And when they [see vs. 27] had fulfilled all things that were written of him, they took him down from the tree, and laid him in a tomb." Here the several actors who caused the death of Christ are grouped together [see vs. 28] with Joseph of Arimathaea, who actually took him down from the tree and laid him in the tomb. A person unacquainted with the narratives of the Gospels would think that they who procured Christ's condemnation buried him also; but Luke did not think so. Joseph was waiting for the kingdom of God, and had not concurred with Christ's enemies; (see Luke xxiii. 50–53, where καθελών and ἔθηκεν are the words used in Acts, only that they are in the singular in the Gospel.)

Another example, which no one could misunderstand, is found in Luke i. 80, "and the child grew and waxed strong in spirit, and was in the deserts till the day of his showing unto Israel." Here the child was, without question, not in the deserts from his infancy upward, but the three predicates are joined together, for brevity's sake, by one subject, τὸ παιδίον.

But to return to the more important peculiarity of Luke which we noticed just above: the first example of it we draw from chapters x. and xi. of the Acts. In chapter x. certain Christian brethren accompany Peter to Caesarea, and the narrative consists of a simple statement of facts, together with the speech of Peter touching the leading points of the gospel. In xi. 12, "certain brethren" are spoken of as "these six brethren," who went to Jerusalem with the apostle, no doubt, to corroborate his words spoken in his own defence. But of more importance is the new matter in xi. 16, where we first learn that Peter's prejudices against baptizing Cornelius gave way on the recollection of the Lord's words (Acts i. 5) respecting the baptism with the Holy Spirit.

Another instance of this peculiarity is found in the threefold narrative of the conversion of Paul. Two of these are given to us as coming in public addresses from the apostle himself. Both of them Luke might well have heard; since he went to Jerusalem with the apostle, where one of them was spoken, and may have been with him at his hearing before Agrippa, as he was certainly with Paul on the voyage to Italy. In the historical narrative (chap. ix.) we find only, "I am Jesus whom thou persecutest," without the words "it is hard for thee to kick against the pricks." These words belong to the speech before Agrippa, and are, without question, intruded into chap. ix. by some harmonizing copyist, but are found in no Greek manuscript.

The remaining new matter in chap. xxvi., besides these

words, is the specification of the time when the vision appeared to Paul. "At midday ..... I saw a light from heaven," and the very important commission to preach the gospel of forgiveness to the Gentiles. In chap. ix. nothing is said of this; but Ananias is told by the Lord Jesus that " Saul is a chosen vessel to carry Christ's name before Gentiles and kings and the children of Israel."

And again, when the speech in chap. xxii. is compared with the narrative in chap. ix. we find several differences, such as that touching the effect of the vision on Paul's companions; the important addition giving an account of the apostle's trance at Jerusalem; and his new commission to preach the gospel to the Gentiles. This last particular, of course, could not appear in chap. ix.; but it shows either the freeness of Luke in treating his materials, or his fidelity in introducing his matter when it came in his hearing from the apostle's lips, or possibly his use of detached portions on what he judged the proper occasion,— all of which portions may have been familiar to him in his long intercourse with Paul. He might have narrated everything in chap. ix.; but he chose, from some reason or other, to reserve it and let it come from the apostle himself.

Another instance, and the last that we shall adduce, of this peculiarity is furnished by comparing Acts xix. 21, 22 with xxiv. 17. From the first passage we learn Paul's purpose to go through Macedonia and Achaia, and that before starting on his journey he had sent two of his helpers to the first mentioned province. From the second passage, it appears that he effected his purpose, and, as he had intended, was soon on his way to Syria (xx. 2, 3), Jerusalem being his objective point. If, now, we possessed no other information in regard to his movements, we should take it to be nothing strange that his tour extended over the countries of Europe where he had planted churches, and that he had the best of reasons for visiting the holy city. On discovering, however, from the Epistles to the Romans (xv. 25-28) and the Corinthians (1 Cor. xvi. 1; 2 Cor. viii.; ix.), that these journeys, aside from the ordinary work of the apostle, had in view the special object of making collections for the poor Christians at Jerusalem, we should wonder at Luke's making no mention of this important object, which in its consequences gave a new turn to Paul's life afterward. But as we read onward from the bare notice (xx. 1, 2) of his visit to Macedonia and Greece, and reach his defence of himself before Felix (xxiv. 17), we find that it is there brought out, in the words, " Now, after many years, I came to bring alms to my nation, and offerings." Luke postpones this mention of Paul's special business at Jerusalem until after he had been through all the trying scenes there, and had been conveyed to Caesarea. He must have had the facts in his mind all the while, as he had come to Jerusalem with the apostle.

Is it possible, after the considerations brought forward in this study, to doubt that Luke was perfectly aware, when he closed his first book, that Christ did not ascend to heaven on the evening of the resurrection day? Is it not quite credible that he made his brief summary of events that took place until after the ascension, with the intention of speaking of them, or of some of them, again in a second narrative, to which they would be an appropriate beginning? And is not the relation of the end of the Gospel and the beginning of the Acts explained by his habit of composition when he felt called to make a renewed mention of the same portion of the evangelical history?

II.

SOME REMARKS ON ACTS I. 1-12, ESPECIALLY ON THE WORD συναλιζόμενος.

The ascension of our Lord is the event which separates between his personal and his spiritual presence in the world. When he committed the interests of the kingdom of heaven on earth directly to his apostles, he left them not alone but promised them the Holy Spirit. This promise was the principal subject of his last words with them before he went to the garden; he repeats it after his resurrection. But when the Spirit was to come and, in a sense, to take his place he did not at once let them know. For a time his plan seems to have been to appear to them as to a whole body, or to portions of them, or to large numbers of believers, or to single persons, in order that the belief in his resurrection might be deeply fixed in their minds. He did not even detain them in Jerusalem during this time of waiting, but suffered them to revisit their homes in Galilee, and recruit themselves, before the great work in Jerusalem should begin. They were, in fact, not yet fitted for their work; and this interval was the time of preparation. It continued forty days; during which, from time to time, he appeared to them, or to some of them, making them sure that he still had an earthly form. Luke's expression is, δι' ἡμερῶν τεσσαράκοντα ὀπτανόμενος αὐτοῖς, that is, "at intervals through forty days making his appearance to them, or letting himself be seen by them." Or as Chrysostom explains it (Op. ix. 18, ed. Migne), "Luke did not say '*forty days*,' but δι' ἡμερῶν τεσσαράκοντα · ἐφίστατο γὰρ, καὶ ἀφίπτατο (or ἀφίστατο) πάλιν." Διά is thus used in Acts v. 19, where an angel of the Lord opens the doors of the prison, διὰ νυκτός; and in Acts xvii. 10, where the disciples sent Paul out from Thessalonica, not *through*, but *at some time in the night, by night*. So in xvi. 9, a vision appeared to Paul, διὰ νυκτός, certainly not continuing through the night. And so in Acts xiii. 31, "who was seen for many days," ἐπί denotes *in a space of time reaching over* many days (cf. xvi. 18). So in Latin *per* is used; as in Sueton. Caes. § 45, "per somnum exterreri solebat," not *through*, but *in* sleep.

Either one or two of these visits of the Lord Jesus are especially noticed by Luke. From verse 6 onwards, the place of his meeting with his apostles was Mount Olivet, which Luke called Bethany in his Gospel; and it is remarkable that he makes in his second narrative (Acts i. 12), no mention of the place, taking it for granted that Theophilus must have remembered what was said in the first narrative (Luke xxiv. 50). It is worthy of notice, also, that he conceives of the apostles' return to Jerusalem as being made towards a common upper room, and that others besides — the women, and Mary the mother of Jesus, and his brethren — were with them. Why should these women come to the feast of Pentecost a number of days beforehand, unless a summons had been sent to them, (either individually by him or by some apostle), from the risen Saviour?

Going back now to verses 4 and 5, we ask whether the meeting of Christ with his apostles there mentioned was the same with that spoken of in verse 6, or, in other words, was it on the *resurrection* day, or was it some earlier meeting at Jerusalem? and what sense are we to give to συναλιζόμενος? The great body of Protestant commentators hold to a reference in verse 6 to verse 4, as speaking of the same gathering. Meyer considers that which is spoken of in verse 6 to be a later meeting on the resurrection day. The Greek interpreters explain συναλιζόμενος as meaning "while taking food with them"; the Latin interpreters, the Vulgate, the Catholic church, and some few Protestants, among whom so able a commentator as Meyer is to be counted, agree with the Greeks. Our Authorized Version and the new revision insert the marginal note "eating with them." It is to these two points that the rest of this study will be devoted.

1. Do verses 4 and 6 refer to the same gathering of Christ and his apostles, or must the narrative of a later day begin at verse 6? This point may be considered without discussing the meaning of the word συναλιζόμενος immediately; for, whether we render it "while *taking meat with*, or *being assembled together with*," in both cases there is a certain abruptness and want of connection between the three first verses and the fourth. We may naturally conceive that "the things pertaining to the kingdom of God" was the leading thought in Luke's mind, and that verse 4, as well as the following ones, bears on that important point. But this Christ would do on occasions when he met with his disciples; and this, without question, was one cause of his remaining on earth. One of these meetings is now spoken of, and is loosely connected with the preceding part of the narrative by καί. But the whole matter turns on verse 6, —

on οἱ μὲν οὖν συνελθόντες ἠρώτων. Here observe, first, that in some passages where μὲν οὖν are found in connection with οἱ and a participle, the οἱ and the participle are together the subject; and in others οἱ is the subject, and the participle expresses the secondary or qualifying notion. Examples of this latter relation between the two occur in Acts viii. 25, "they, therefore, when they had testified and spoken"; in xv. 30; xxiii. 31, and in the present instance. In xvii. 30; xxiii. 22; xxvi. 4, 9, there is no associated participle (ὁ μὲν οὖν χιλίαρχος, τοὺς μὲν οὖν χρόνους, τὴν μὲν οὖν βίωσίν μου, ἐγὼ μὲν οὖν). In the example in verse 6, the sense is not *they who came together*, but οἱ alone is the subject: "*they, therefore*, when they came together," not, as De Wette takes it, "Die nun so zusammen gekommen waren." For the formula μὲν οὖν cf. A. Buttmann, § 149, 16. Οὖν evidently refers back to verse 4, or rather to αὐτοῖς in verse 4; and verse 4 itself is shown, by being placed after the mention of the appearances of Christ through forty days, not to refer to the evening of the resurrection day. When, therefore, we notice the connection between verses 4 and 6, we can hardly help believing that the apostles came together, by appointment or direct suggestion to their minds, as in the case recorded by Matthew (xxviii. 16), τὸ ὄρος, οὗ ἐτάξατο αὐτοῖς ὁ Ἰησοῦς. They had not remained in Jerusalem since the week after the crucifixion; but now, when the outpouring of the Spirit was at hand, they are summoned to meet the Lord for the last time on earth. Συνελθόντες implies that they were scattered before, — and we may suppose that they were summoned from their old homes in Galilee, and with them the women, who might not have gone to the pentecostal feast on ordinary occasions. The time of this convention was the morning of the ascension day.

2. But what is the meaning of συναλιζόμενος? In order to answer this question we must draw upon our reader's patience, for the word has a very curious history which cannot be dispatched in a few words.

There are three verbs in Greek having the common form

ἀλίζω, two of them beginning with ἀ, and the other with ἁ. Ἁλίζω or ἁλίω, a rare word, meaning *to roll*, is represented in the classics by the derivatives, ἁλινδέω, ἁλινδήθρα (rolling place for horses); and ἐξαλίσας, ἐξήλικα, the three last of which occur in Aristophanes. With this we have no concern. Of the other two, ἀλίζω, *collect together*, with its compound, συναλίζω,[1] in good use from Herodotus downward, has a common origin with ἀλής, *confertus*, with ἁλία (some ἡλία), an *assembly*, or gathering, and with ἡλιαία, a place where the Athenian dikasts first met, whence they are called Heliasts.

The words ἀλίζω, συναλίζω, *collect, assemble*, with no more difference of sense than their more common synonymes, ἀθροίζω, συναθροίζω, appeared first in Empedocles, Herodotus, and Hippocrates, and stood their ground down to the latest period of Greek literary composition; although the explanation of them in glossaries and lexica seems to show that they were not terms of common life in later times. There are sixteen instances of them in Herodotus, four in Hippocrates, one in a fragment of Empedocles, several in Xenophon, one in Plato (Cratylus, 409 A), and two in Euripides. Aristophanes has συναλιάζω, a Doric equivalent to συναλίζω.[2] Some of the later writers who use one or the other of them are Josephus, Antiq. xix. 7,8; 9, 4; Lucian, De Luctu, chap. 7; Appian, Hispan. § 61, de B. C. i. § 132; iv. 65; v. 140; Plutarch de Plac. Philos. (902), where it is said that in the process of sifting, things such as seeds, ἐπὶ τὸ αὐτὸ συναλίζεται, so that in sifting, beans and chick-peas, in a body, take different places. So again Jamblichus (in Vit. Pythag.) speaks of a class of persons "who gather together for the sake of sight-seeing," συναλιζόμενον τόπων θέας ἕνεκα; and Athenaeus, lib. ii. p. 40, C., explains θαλία by the fact that θεῶν χάριν ἡλίζοντο; intending to say, if I understand his words, that it was composed of θεὸς and ἁλία, denoting a sacred banquet. The verb ἀλίζω

---

[1] Other compounds, ἀναλίζω (see below) and ἐξαλίζω, a conjecture of Valckenaer, Schol. in Nov. Test., p. 301, perhaps had no existence.

[2] Comp. Ahrens de Gr. Ling. Dialectis, lib. ii. p. 90.

occurs also in Theodoret, Hist. iii. 1 and iii. 15. For other passages where ἁ. or συνα. occurs in ecclesiastical writers, comp. Sophocles (lexicon, s. v.). I have noticed συνάλισις, which is not to be found in the common lexicons, in the life of Nicephorus by Ignatius (de Boor's Niceph. Opusc. Lips. 188).

Nowhere does a middle form of ἁλίζ. or συναλίζ. *colligo*, occur, although many interpreters have regarded the participle in Acts i. 4 as belonging to the middle voice of this verb.[1] In fact, no such form was needed, since the passives of a number of verbs, meaning *to gather*, freely take a neuter or deponent signification in Greek ; so in Latin, *congregor* is neuter in such examples as Tacitus, Ann. i. 30. Nor need we go beyond the New Testament for parallel instances. Συνάγω is so used in John xviii. 2 (and Jesus πολλάκις συνήχθη ἐκεῖ, etc.), and in other places noticed by Grimm s.v. So also Josephus says, (de Bel. Jud. vi. 6), πολλοὶ καὶ συνείκοσιν ἀθροίζονται, " they assemble twenty together," to eat the passover.

Besides this ἁλίζω, there is another similar form from ἅλς, denoting *to salt*, or *to make salt, to give salt to*, in which last sense Aristotle uses it in his Hist. Animal. viii. 10. In the other sense it occurs in the New. Test. twice or three times, in Matt. v. 13, and in Mark ix. 49, where some authorities insert it twice. In the Septuagint it is found in Lev. ii. 13, to which one of the examples in Mark seems to refer. It is found also in Ezek. xvi. 4, οὐδὲ ἁλὶ ἡλίσθης, and in Isa. li. 6, in the version of Symmachus, who mistook the meaning of his original. Another passage is found in Ezra (iv. 14), which the Septuagint entirely leaves out, but which the Complutensian edition gives us in a translation of the Hebrew, by καὶ νῦν οὖν καθὼς ἅλας τοῦ ναοῦ ἡλισάμεθα (where ναοῦ stands for the Hebrew word הֵיכַל, here denoting *palace*, and which the margin of King James's version correctly renders), " we are salted with the salt of the palace " = *we receive the king's salt*, or salary.

[1] Comp. συναλισάμενον in Manetho, below, which cannot be from this verb.

A compound verb directly derived from ἁλίζω, *to salt*, has evaded my search. There is, however, as I must believe, a rare verb συναλίζομαι in the middle voice, tracing its paternity to σύναλος, *taking salt with*, which Philoxenus has preserved in a gloss (Eng. ed. of Stephanus, vol. viii.), and explains by *consalineus*, a Latin word of equal rarity. From this a middle or deponent form may be readily derived, denoting *the taking of salt*, or a meal, *with another*.[1]

The quantity of the *a* in these forms deserves notice. Ἅλς and its derivatives have a short alpha; ἁλής, ἁλίζω, *colligo*, and words connected with them, a long alpha, with the exception of ἅλις. This is expressly asserted in the Etymol. Mag. ed. Sturz. (marginal page 61, line 50), and is confirmed by a line of Empedocles which Macrobius cites (Saturnal. i. 17), where Macrobius says that " the sun is called ἥλιος ὅτι συναλισθέντος πολλοῦ πυρὸς περιπολεῖ, ut ait Empedocles, οὕνεκ' ἀναλισθεὶς μέγαν οὐρανον ἀμφιπολεύει." The sense of the verse is that, because consisting of collected or conglobated fire, he travels round the great heaven. Sturz in his Empedocles and in his ed. of the Etymol. Mag. alters this into ἀλλ' ὁ μὲν ἀλισθεὶς etc., but the quantity is not thereby affected. A later testimony to the length of the *a* in ἁλίζω, *colligo*, is given by Euripides, Herc. Fur. 411, 412, compared with the antistrophe, 428, 429, where βίοτον οὐδ' ἔβα πάλιν answers to ἄγορον ἁλίσας φίλων. Accordingly, in the Heraclidae, v. 404, where Scaliger and Barnes read συναλίσας, Musgrave and Elmsley put into the text εἰς ἓν ἁλίσας, which suits the end of a trimeter better, and is received by later scholars.[2]

The interest of this discussion, as far as passages in the

---

[1] Thus εὐθήμων, εὐθημονέομαι, Plato (the active is quite late); εὐλαβής, εὐλαβέομαι; συνεδρία, συνεδριάομαι; σύνοφρυς, συνοφρυόομαι. But the examples are not numerous. The derivation is easier from σύναλος, as far as the sense is concerned, than from συν-αλίζω, and no συναλίζω, *I take salt with*, is found.

[2] Ἁλής has a long alpha in a fragment of Callimachus (in No. 86 of Bentley's Coll., ed. Ernesti, ii. 458), in a choliambic verse. In a corrupt fragment of Hesiod preserved by Strabo (vii. p. 322), ἐκ γαίης ἀλέους, *a* would be short if ἀλέας were the true reading, but modern editors of Strabo have altered it into ἐκ γαίης λάους.

Scriptures are concerned, lies in the word συναλισθῶ of an anonymous translator of Ps. cxli. 4, preserved in Origen's Hexapla (Migne's Origen, vi. 1133), and in Acts i. 4,— mainly in the latter. In the Psalm, where Symmachus and our version give the correct meaning, the Sept. according to the Cod. Alex. has οὐ μὴ συνδυάσω μετὰ τῶν ἐκλεκτῶν αὐτῶν, the Cod. Vat. has συνδοιάσω, and the Sinaitic, ἐνδοιάσω; which last reading looks like a copyist's blunder. Symmachus has μὴ συμφάγοιμι τὰ ἡδέα, and the anonymous translator, μὴ συναλισθῶ ἐν ταῖς τερπνότησιν αὐτῶν. The sense here seems to be, *may I not gather with them at their delights*, or delicacies. The translation *may I not eat with*, however, has been given to the word here, which is wholly improbable; for if συναλίζομαι *eat with*, exists, it is certainly found in the first aorist middle, and a word in so little use would not be likely to have the passive and the middle aorist forms both. The Syriac has a form from a root answering to the Hebrew מלח, *I will not eat salt with*, or, possibly, to make a covenant with (?); while the Hebrew has לחם, *eat with*.

The early translations seem to follow the Septuagint. Thus the Old Latin, as given by Sabatier from two MSS., is *combinabo*, and Augustine in his enarratio of Ps. cxl. (cxli.) *combinabor*, explaining the passage of the wicked, "cum quibus non est habenda societas." Jerome gives the sense of the Septuagint in the words of the Vulgate, "non communicabo cum electis suorum." The interpretation of Theodoret is ἐμοὶ μὴ εἴη τις πρὸς αὐτοὺς κοινωνία. We have thus a singular puzzle. How came the Septuagint to give συνδυάσω, which must mean *pair* or *join with*, for the Hebrew verb denoting *to eat?* This word probably determined the word συναλισθῶ of the anonymous translator; and yet the Syriac may be appealed to, in connection with Symmachus, to show that the translator meant *may I not eat with*. All the Greek versions mistake in respect to the word rendered *dainties* or delicacies. Whether any further light may be shed on this point, I know not; but it is altogether most probable that συναλισθῶ is from συναλίζω, *colligo*. The translator took the word denoting *to gather* or *assemble with*, and expressed the sense which, as he thought, belonged to the text, that of meeting with persons in their festivities.

But are there any other instances of the occurrence of συναλίζομαι, *comedo*, in the Greek language? I must believe that there are two, one of them belonging to the second, and the other to the fifth, century of our era. Besides these there are none to be found, unless in quite late periods; and I have fallen upon no trace of these, if there are any. One tolerably, if not altogether, clear example of such a verb in such a sense is found in Manetho's astrological poems. These productions, composed under the Roman empire, are divided into three portions: the first, consisting of the second, third, and sixth books, was written, according to the most recent editor, Köchly, not before M. Antoninus nor after Alexander Severus, and probably in the reign of the latter (between A.D. 138 and 235); the fourth book must have been written before Valens, who died in 378; while the first and fifth books of the old editions, called the fifth and sixth by Köchly, were written after the fourth, thus belonging to the end of the fourth or to the fifth century.[1] The passage containing the word from συναλίζομαι occurs just at the end of Köchly's sixth, or the older editor's fifth, book. The author is speaking of a woman born under the conjunction of certain heavenly bodies, and says that she will be πῆμα λυγρῷ γαμετῇ συναλιζόμενον κακοῆθες. The Latin translator renders the participle by *congregans*; being ignorant, it would seem, that the short alpha demands a derivation of the word from ἅλς. If, then, any word from that root existed, this must be referred to it; unless the author or authors, whom Köchly declares to be " ignorantia metrorum et ingenii stupore simillimos," mistoook the quantity of the second syllable. We have seen that the same error in regard to metre was found in the early text of Euripides, but the sense and measure concur in favoring the derivation from ἅλς.

---

[1] Compare Köchly's preface to his Didot edition, pp. vi, xvii, xl. The same recension appears in a small volume of the Teubner Series of Greek writers.

The only other instance hitherto adduced where συναλίζομαι, *eat with*, is to be found, occurs in the Clementines; not in the passage from the sixth Homily which Meyer cites, — where nothing of the kind is to be found, unless it be ἁλῶν μεταλαβεῖν, at the end of the Homily, — but in a passage repeated in Homily xiii. § 4, and in the two Epitomes, the older of which appears in Cotelerius, and the new one, almost identical with it, was published by Dressel from an Ottobonian MS. of the Vatican. Besides these three places, which are but three forms of a single original, συναλίζομαι is used in the epistle of Clement to James, which precedes the Homilies (§ 15), in the old classical sense.

Beginning with this last mentioned place, we find the Christians to be there compared to persons on the deep. They are told to expect all manner of afflictions, as sailing on the great and troubled sea, which is the world; being sometimes despondent, persecuted, hungry, thirsty, naked, scattered, in great straits; sometimes, again, united, collected together, enjoying quiet (καὶ πάλιν ὅτε μὲν ἑνούμενοι, συναλιζόμενοι, ἡσυχάζοντες). Another reading, which Dressel prefers, is συναυλιζόμενοι, a common word which is intruded into the text in the three other places presently to be examined, as well as in Acts i. 4, and elsewhere. The reading given above is plainly best suited to the context, being demanded by σκορπιζόμενοι in the previous part of the sentence. And in the free translation attributed to Rufinus (in Migne's Clement, under the text), — quippe qui et dispergendos se nonnunquam noverint, sed aliquando etiam congregandos," — the same reading is supported.

Putting this passage out of account, we come to the three others. In them all Peter tells Clement's mother that, so long as she is a heathen and unbaptized, she cannot eat with the Christians. Even relatives for that reason must be separated at table. But when they are baptized, τότε δὴ αὐτοῖς καὶ συναλιζόμεθα (συναυλ. in Epit. 1., τότε αὐτοῖς according to Epit. 2 and Hom. xiii. § 4). It might be claimed, possibly, that the sense of Epit. 1 is *then we even lodge with them*, i.e. not only take food, but lodge. But this cannot be the sense or the reading. For here the Recognitiones will show how Rufinus understood the disputed word, and that he read συναλ., not συναυλ. The passage is translated by Rufinus from a text of the lost ἀναγνωρίσεις, or *Recognitiones*, closely similar to that of the Epitomes and the Homily. We transcribe a part of it from Gersdorf's edition of the Recognitiones (Lib. vii. § 29, p. 167) : " Sed et illud observamus, mensam cum gentilibus non habere communem [in Hom. and Epit. τραπέζης ἐθνικῆς μὴ μετέχειν], nisi cum crediderint et recepta veritate baptizati fuerint, ac [?] trina quadam beati nominis invocatione consecrati; et tunc cum eis cibum sumimus [Hom. and Epit. συναλιζόμεθα, with the variant συναυλ., as before]. Alioquin etiam si pater aut mater sint, aut uxor aut filii aut fratres, non possumus cum eis mensam habere communem [συνεστιᾶσθαι]. Quia ergo religionis causa praecipua hoc facimus, non tibi injuriosum videatur, quod non potest filius tuus una tecum sumere cibum [τὸ μὴ συνεστιᾶσθαί σοι], usquequo eadem tibi sit quae illi sententia fidei."

It is almost certain that Rufinus, who has the words "cum eis cibum sumimus" in his text, must have there found συναλιζόμεθα, and not συναυλιζόμεθα. And that he thought that there were two verbs with the same letters is shown by the translation given on another page, *congregandos*, to the word συναλιζομένους occurring in the letter of James to Clement, — if the translation there given be really his.

The force of the argument from the sanction given to the meaning *eat with* by Rufinus might be broken by showing that the word συναλ. with this sense was a late interloper into the Greek language. We regard this to be quite possible; but as the time of its entrance into the Greek language cannot be shown; and as it certainly was in existence before the Clementines were written in the second century of our era, and before or as soon as the Old Latin versions of the New Testament appeared, it might easily have imposed upon the more ignorant of the early translators.

But may there not be force in a remark of Casaubon (in his Animadv. in Athen. ii. ch. 3) on a passage of Athenaeus already cited (supra p. 606). The great scholar there says, " Etsi ἁλίζεσθαι et συναλίζεσθαι generali notione congregari significant, sine finis discrimine, fuere tamen qui de convenientibus ad coenam condictam proprie putarent usurpari. Ita usus est Athenaeus illa voce." Here it is noticeable that Casaubon was not acquainted with the argument for two verbs, identical in form, from the length of the alpha. And, moreover, the derivation of θαλία from θεὸς-ἁλία would not now be thought to deserve attention. Valckenaer, however, in his Scholae in Act. Apostol. (Select. e Schol. Valck. i. 362, Amstel. 1815) follows Casaubon in his view of the meaning of the participle, besides adopting the reading συναλιζομένοις proposed by Hemsterhuis. " Because," says he, " those who used a common table were said ἁλῶν μεταλαβεῖν, hinc factum ut ἁλίζεσθαι et συναλίζ. coeperint in usu significare *in unum locum congregari cibi capiendi gratia*. Et hinc manifestum erit cur vetus interpres Latinus reddideret *convescens*." But he prefers the reading of Hemsterhuis, and understands it of the sacred supper. But in his Opuscula (ii. 277) he rejects the conjecture συναλιζομένοις, because the Christian Fathers found the nominative in their copies, and understood the word as denoting *familiariter cum aliquo vivere, ejusdem mensae participem; salem simul edere*, and supposes without reason that Peter's words in Acts x. 40, 41 are to be explained by this passage. He also refers to the Clementines (Hom. xiii. § 4) as supporting the same use of the word. But he does not seem to affirm positively that two words from two different roots existed.

We come now, in the next place, to the inquiry how far the word συναλίζομαι, *eat with*, is recognized in the ancient lexica and glossaries. The answer must be that for the greater part they make no mention of such a word, and seem not to know that it exists. They generally explain ἁλίζω, *colligo* and συναλίζω by ἀθροίζω, συναθροίζω, and συνάγω. Thus Photius, Hesychius, Suidas. In Hesychius we notice that συναλισθείς, συναθροισθείς, and συναχθείς serve to interpret συναλιζόμενος, which leads to a suspicion that the present in Acts i. 4 is thus explained by the aorist. In the Onomastikon of Julius Pollux, among the words for partaking of food this does not appear, as was remarked long ago by Erasmus. In the Etymologica, the Magnum and Gudianum, we find ξυναλιζόμενοι or ξυναυλιζόμενοι explained by συναθροιζόμενοι ἢ συνεσθίοντες, and then παρὰ τοὺς ἅλας is added to show how it could be synonymous with συνεσθίοντες.

Coming to the works of Christian writers, we fail to find in those of the ante-Nicene age any reference to the word as occurring in our text, or to the verse itself. Luke xxiv. 37–39 is cited by Tertullian (Adv. Marcion., iv. § 43), and Acts x. 41 is cited in the Ignatian epistle to the church at Smyrna. And may it not be fairly argued that if the meaning of *eating with* had been already fastened on this word we should have known of it by more than one citation of that early period?

There can, however, be no question that such a sense was attached to it some time in the second century. The early Latin expresses the word by *vescor*, or by *convescor*, which Jerome adopted. Another word translating it into Latin is *conversor*, which seems to point towards συναυλιζόμενος. *Simul convivens* appears in the Cod. Bezae (D) although D itself has συναλισκόμενος in this place. In the Latin version of the Cod. Laudianus (E of Acts) *vescens* appears; with which the venerable Bede agrees, who, as Dr. Scrivener, after Dr. Mill, thinks (Introd. 2d ed. p. 147), must have had this manuscript before him when he wrote his Expositio Retractata of the Acts. The Eastern versions seem all to agree with the Greek interpreters of the post-Nicene period in rendering this word by some equivalent to partaking of food.

After the Nicene period the authority of Chrysostom and others helped the general spread of this explanation. Chrysostom refers to Acts i. 4 in at least five different passages. It occurs twice in the first Homily on Acts (§§ 3, 6, Op. Chr. ed. Migne, ix.), three times in that in Princip. Act. iv. (§§ 104, 107, Migne iii. 1). In the first passage he says:

"Nor was he [Luke] content with the forty days, but he adds also a table, in reference to which, as he proceeds, he uses the words καὶ συναλιζόμενος αὐτοῖς. And this the apostles always regard as a proof of the resurrection." Again, in § 6 Chrysostom says (p. 22 ed. Migne), "Inasmuch, then, as we take food with Christ, and have a common table with him [συναλιζόμενοι Χριστῷ καὶ τραπέζης κοινωνοῦντες]"; where he evidently refers to this passage, although he is speaking of Christian baptism. In the other three places he explains the word by κοινωνῶν τραπέζης, or by τραπέζης only, or by οὐ δεόμενος τραπέζης ἔτρωγεν. The word is constantly interpreted by him, as if the people did not understand it.

Theophylact on Acts i. 4 says that in a space of forty days αὐτοῖς συνηλίζετο κοινωνῶν ἁλῶν καὶ κοινωνῶν τραπέζης, where he arbitrarily joins συναλ. with forty days, and conceives of Christ as partaking of food with the apostles through that period; whereas the word is used of a single event. Oecumenius gives the same explanation, which is found also in the Panarion of Epiphanius (in Haeres. 66, § 35, and probably in Haeres. 20, § 3). Theodoret, again,— who, as we have seen, uses the word συναλ., *colligo*,— gives the sense of *eating with* to it in this passage in the Dialogue Inconfusus (ed. Sirmond-Schultze, iv. 119). After citing the first words of vs. 4, he adds that Peter more distinctly says, "'We who eat and drank with him after he rose from the dead' (Acts x. 41). For," continues Theodoret, "since to eat is a peculiarity of those who have to do with the present life, the Lord of necessity proved his resurrection to those who hold not the truth by eating and drinking." And this he supports by Christ's ordering something to be given to the daughter of Jairus, and by having Lazarus, whom he raised from the dead, his companion at a feast.

We reach the conclusion that there was a verb identical in form with the passive or middle of συναλίζω, *colligo*, of late origin as far as can be known, and of extremely limited use. The importance given to it by esteemed and learned Fathers does not seem to have given it any currency; at least, I cannot find that it went down into the Middle Ages. Sophocles in his lexicon has no place for it, and I cannot find it in modern Greek lexicons. It seems very improbable that Luke should have used such a word.

But why did he use συναλιζόμενος, *assembling with*, when the verb occurs nowhere else in his writings or in the New Testament, and so many synonymes were at hand? I am unable to give an answer; unless, possibly, it was associated in the evangelist's mind with the *collecting* or *mustering* of the apostles — a sense which it has in the classics. But no answer is due to those who would discover in this form a word of the very greatest rarity.

The use of the present participle is Meyer's principal argument against giving the sense of *gathering* to the word; while if we could translate it *taking bread with them*, the tense would be all right. But the verb in the passive with a deponent meaning can denote, if I mistake not, both the transitory act of being assembled or meeting with another, and the permanent condition of being in a meeting; so that συναλιζόμενος = ὅτε συνηλίζετο might be used here without grammatical difficulty. A somewhat parallel passage, in this respect, occurs at the very end of the Iliad:

εὖ συναγειρόμενοι δαίνυντ᾽ ἐρικυδέα δαῖτα

where the modern editions since Heyne have generally preferred this reading to συναγειράμενοι.

It seems harsh in English to speak of a single person being assembled, or having been assembled, with others. But this need not trouble us in Greek, at least in the Greek of the New Testament. Thus Jesus συνήχθη μετὰ τῶν μαθητῶν αὐτοῦ (John xviii. 2), which our English translators render *resort*, perhaps to avoid harshness of expression.

It may be, also, that the substitution by early interpreters of the meaning *eating with* for *being assembled with* had reasons of its own. The passage in Luke xxiv. 42–53, by disregarding the marks of time, may have led many to think that the narrations in Acts i. 4 and Luke xxiv. 49 were identical. This, when the word συναλίζομαι, *eat with*, was discovered, helped to establish a false harmony. And Acts x. 41 aided in giving currency to this meaning, which the word in Luke was not conceived to have from the beginning. The text thus became — honestly on the part of the interpreters — a convenient ally to those other texts which established the human, sensuous nature of our Lord, against heretics, who denied it or made as little of it as possible.

A somewhat subjective difficulty which some persons cannot fail to find in the interpretation of συναλ. by *eating with*, and which we share in, is this: As vs. 4 is closely joined with vs. 6, and vs. 6 points to the day of the ascension, it must follow that our Lord took food on the very day of that great event. But as his taking food after the resurrection is clearly intended to be a proof of his being in a body (comp. Luke xxiv. 41, 42), the reason for his so doing had already ceased. No one doubted who he was when they were assembled in Jerusalem or at Mount Olivet. It seems thus to have then become uncalled for and gratuitous.

We have finished our proposed task, except that we had intended to prepare, and had actually prepared at some length, a sketch of the history of the interpretations of this passage, which would be chiefly confined to the opinions of Protestant commentators, since Jerome's *convescens* has held the Catholic church in fetters. It is singular, however, that a Catholic, Laurentius Valla, the celebrated humanist, first broached a new opinion respecting Acts i. 4 and the word συναλιζόμενος. Erasmus adopted his opinion, and since his time Protestants have very generally given up the early explanation. But they have not all been successful in their treatment of the word. Some, as Calvin and Erasmus, — the latter doubtingly, since he translated it by *congregans se cum illis*, and by *congregans illos in idem loci*, — resort to the middle voice for an interpretation of the word. Others neglect the tense, which creates the difficulty. Rosenmüller has *quum congregasset*, as if it were an aorist; with whom, in substance, Bloomfield (*having gathered together*), Heinrichs (in Köppen's New Testament), Kuinöl, and Olshausen agree; several of whom also regard it as in the middle. Other opinions may be found in the Critici Sacri, or in J. C. Wolff's Curae Philologicae. Bengel has *conventum agens;* a considerable number, *conveniens cum illis,* its equivalent; to which two latter renderings there can be no objection. De Wette gives *indem er mit ihnen versammelt ward,* and remarks that Theophylact in his interpretation κοινωνῶν ἁλῶν followed a false etymology. Alford follows this remark, without giving any interpretation in English. Plumptre, in Ellicott's series, thinks that Jerome's *convescens* rests on a mistaken etymology. But the question of sense precedes that of etymology, provided two words with the same form existed. Jacobson, in the Speaker's Commentary, notices the marginal reading of the Authorized Version, and simply states that Josephus assigns to the word the meaning preferred in the text. Howson, in Schaff's Popular Commentary, goes back to the signification *eating with* of the margin, and thinks the authority of Chrysostom with his followers, and of Jerome, decisive in the matter. Thus in the latest commentary the new direction given by Meyer is accepted, and some others have followed the same able leader. Whether it shall be thought that we have given good reasons for a different judgment or not, this will be the most remarkable instance in which a word nearly unknown to the Greek language, not even mentioned by modern lexicographers either of classical or of New Testament Greek — (the Paris ed. of Stephanus, Robinson, Grimm), has found a footing in the exegetical works and the versions of more than one church. You may search for it in the early times, and you find it everywhere; you may search for it in Greek, outside of this passage, and except in two obscure authors you find it nowhere.

We close this Article with a very brief statement of the order of events as they seem to arrange themselves after the second Lord's day succeeding his resurrection.

1. The apostles returned to Galilee. There they had the interview with Christ recorded in John xxi. At this time,

also, the great gathering with the body of the Galilean disciples may have taken place, "as Jesus had appointed."

2. By a similar appointment, forty days after the resurrection, he met at Jerusalem the apostles and some others of his nearest friends, especially the most devoted Christian women, with his mother and his brethren. We have already remarked that the presence of these female Christians at the feast of pentecost, and so long before the feast, is fully accounted for by a summons from the Lord.

3. The events between vs. 4 and vs. 12 all occurred on ascension day, and from this time it was that they waited for the promise of the Spirit to be fulfilled, which should begin the spread of the new kingdom of Christ.

ARTICLE II.

THE DEVELOPMENT OF MONOTHEISM AMONG THE GREEKS.

BY DR. EDWARD ZELLER. — TRANSLATED FROM THE GERMAN BY EDWIN D. MEAD.

THE subject with which the present Article has to deal has claims upon our interest from more than one side. If it is a grateful task, in and for itself, to follow the history of the human mind in one of its highest relations and among one of the most cultured peoples, the attraction of the task is greatly enhanced if it is connected with other questions of the most universal importance. And this is precisely the case in the present instance. The history of religion has to do with no more important fact, none which takes deeper hold of the spiritual and moral life of mankind, than the origin of monotheism and the rise of Christianity, but also none the thorough historical understanding of which is attended with greater difficulties. It is then fortunate that we meet, in a people so well known as the Greeks, a process which offers for the one of these facts — the genesis of monotheistic faith —

at least an analogy; while, at the same time, it contains one of the essential presuppositions by which the other — the origin of Christianity — is historically conditioned. If we see how the faith in the unity of the divine nature was developed among the Greeks from polytheism, we shall likewise find more comprehensible the same faith among other peoples,— even though it may have made its appearance among these in another way and under other conditions; and if Christianity found a definite form of this faith already existing in the province of Hellenic culture, we shall be able the more easily to explain how it could not only conquer the Hellenic portion of the old world in a comparatively short time, but also how it could itself become what it is.

The Greek religion was originally, as is well known, and like all natural religions, polytheism. But the human spirit cannot long rest satisfied with the mere multiplicity of divine natures. The empirical connection of all phenomena, and the need of a fixed moral order in the world, early necessitate the reduction of the multiplicity, in some way, to unity. We find, therefore, in all religions which have only worked themselves in some measure out of the first rude condition the faith in a supreme divinity, a king of gods, who is commonly not thought of as simply dwelling in the heavens, but is really the all-embracing heaven itself. And the world of Greek divinities, so far as our knowledge extends, is brought to a point of unity in Zeus, the lightning-launching god of heaven. The nature of this god, however, appears in the older popular faith, as the Homeric and Hesiodic poems represent it, to be limited in a threefold relation. In the first place, he has above him the dark power of Fate, to which he has to subject himself, against his will and with grievous complaint, as at the death of his son Sarpedon, when he cries: "Woe is me, woe, now Fate wills that Sarpedon, to me dearest of men, shall be slain by Patroclus, the son of Menoetius." Further, he has beside him, in the other Olympians, a rather insubordinate aristocracy, to which he is, indeed, decidedly superior in force and sovereignty, but which in particular things not rarely contradicts or circumvents him, disturbs his plans, and puts hinderances in the way of their execution. To this double limitation, however, Zeus is subject, in the third place, only because his nature is in itself limited, because he is not yet endowed with the entire fulness of that spiritual and moral perfection which, where it is once received as indispensable in the conception of Deity, immediately excludes every thought of a limitation of the divine power.

The Homeric Zeus is, indeed, a moral being, — the protector of right, the avenger of crime, the shield of states, the source of law and custom on earth, the father of gods and men. But, aside also from the fact that the divine rule of the world is not here free from despotic arbitrariness, — that Zeus has two vessels in his store-room, as the proverb goes, one of good things and the other of evil, and deals out according to his discretion, — what judgment must a thoughtful Greek of the subsequent time have passed upon the king of the gods, who, now in Here's arms, now with mortal women, forgets the affairs of his government; who afflicts men with evils of every sort because Prometheus had deceived him in the sacrifice; who dooms the Achaian army to defeats to please Thetis; who sends a deceiving dream to Agamemnon, in order to animate him for the combat, etc.? The weaknesses of sensuous and finite nature appear far too glaringly in these old Greek gods, and even in the highest god, to allow the germ of a higher conception, — which surely is not lacking even in the Homeric theology, — to come to development without a thorough-going change; and if the most offensive narrations are to be interpreted in great part as the personification of existences and forces of nature, — the transformation of natural events into a history of the gods, — this origin of the myths was still hidden from the consciousness of the Greek people itself; to this they appeared with the claim to be a faithfully true delineation of the divine world. In the mysteries, too, which in modern times have been not seldom regarded as the school of a purer religious faith, such a faith is surely not to be found; as, indeed, it is in and for itself a strange idea that in the worship of Demeter or of Dionysius a monotheistic creed could have been communicated. This secret service, moreover, first attained a higher significance for the life of the Greek people after the sixth century, i.e. precisely from the time in which the gradual purification of the popular faith and its approach to monotheism began.

This purification was accomplished in two ways: on the one hand, the representations of Zeus and his government of the world were elevated and refined, and thus the monotheistic element, which lay in polytheism itself without deranging its foundations, was elevated, the polytheistic element being subordinated to it. On the other hand, the multiplicity of gods and the anthropomorphism with which the popular faith had environed the gods were opposed. In the first of these ways the poets worked, seeking to improve the mythology at the very time it was most complete. The philosophers united with this the second way; and from this union proceeded that more spiritual faith, which, extending itself from the time of Socrates and Plato in ever widening circles, had become, wherever the influence of the Hellenic mind reached, the religion of the cultured classes before the appearance of Christianity.

Poetic imagination created the Greek gods and the mythical history of the gods; and it was for the most part the poets by whom this mythology, so readily answering all their wishes and adapting itself with such charming facility, was perfected and fostered. But it was also these same poets who transformed and ennobled it, removed the too rude features, filled the traditions of the olden time with the moral perceptions of more highly educated centuries. Indeed, the great poets of the Greeks were at the same time their first thinkers, the "wise men," as they are so often called, the oldest and most popular teachers of the nation. This idealizing must needs touch, first of all, the figure of Zeus, in which, to the Hellene, everything great and sublime, all his highest conceptions of sovereign power and wisdom, of cosmic regulation and moral order, were condensed. But the higher Zeus was placed, the more completely the mythical anthropomorphisms fell back behind the idea of a perfect being, a righteous, gracious, omniscient ruler of the world; the more completely, too, was monotheism developed from polytheism.

The older poets had, indeed, as we have remarked, praised Zeus as the guardian of right, the representative of moral laws. What Homer and Hesiod had said in this connection, the later poets repeat with stronger emphasis. Zeus beholds, as we read in Archilochus (700 B.C.), the deeds of men, the just and the godless; indeed, the wickedness and the uprightness of the animals do not escape his notice. We must commit all things to his hands. He is, as Terpander says a little later, the beginning and the guide of all. He has, as Simonides of Amorgos sings, the end of all things in his hand, and orders all things as he will. But the further we descend in time, the more strongly do we see this thought developed. Zeus gradually becomes exclusively the supporter of a moral order of the world, the idea of which is freed from the gloom of the old belief in fate, and from the caprice of arbitrary tyranny. Fate, which according to older representation stood behind and above him, melts into unity with his will; the other gods, who still in Homer oppose his purposes in so many ways, become willing instruments of his world-ruling activity. Thus even Solon (590 B.C) teaches us that Zeus watches over all things, and punishes all wickedness; but that he does not fly into a passion over single things, like a man, but suffers wrong to heap itself up before the punishment breaks in. So, a hundred years later, the Sicilian poet, Epicharmus, sings: " Nothing escapes the eye of Deity, of that mayest thou be sure; it is God who watches over us, and to whom nothing is impossible."

Still more decidedly does this purer idea of God appear in the three great poets whose lives fill the period from the last third of the sixth till toward the end of the fifth century,—

Pindar, Aeschylus, and Sophocles. Everything comes from the Deity alone, says Pindar; Zeus sends to mortals everything which happens to them; he grants success, and sends misfortune; he is able to let clear light spring from black night, and to veil the pure brightness of day in thick darkness. Nothing that man does is hidden from Deity; only when it points out the way is blessing to be hoped for; in its hand lies the result of our labor; from it alone spring all virtue and wisdom. In the same sense speaks Aeschylus. The sublimity and omnipotence of Deity, the inevitable fulfilment, the crushing power, of its judgment are impressed by all his tragedies. What Zeus says is done; his will is infallibly accomplished; no mortal has any power against him; none can escape his decrees. The other gods all act in his service; his dominion is also acknowledged in the end, in voluntary submission, by the most opposed powers, even by the titanic defiance of a Prometheus. These thoughts have with Aeschylus such deep and prevailing significance that it would not be difficult, in spite of the polytheistic faith as to which this man of antique honor — this man of Marathon and Salamis — had no doubts, to gather from his poems, with little change of form, the ground features of a pure and lofty monotheism. That which stands before all else in these works is the idea of the divine justice. If even Aeschylus is not yet entirely free from the ancient conception of a jealousy in the Deity, — if we still also read in him that God inflicts misfortunes upon mortals as the very means of working their utter ruin, — the ruling tenor of his works leads us, nevertheless, to recognize the connection of misfortune with guilt, the high justice of the divine judgment. As the man acts, so must he suffer. He whose heart and hand are pure moves sorrowless through life; but retribution surely comes upon the wicked, now with a sudden stroke, now with slow pressure. The Erinnyes control the fate of men; they drain the vital powers of the criminal; they cling without rest to the soles of his feet; they throw around him the snare of madness; they follow his track to the very grave. But the divine grace, even with Aeschylus, is able to overcome the strength of the penal law, and even an Orestes is, in the end, freed from the curse with which matricide had loaded him. In this Aeschylus is, indeed, conscious that he transcends the original character of the Greek religion; but with a most noteworthy, and deeply poetical turn, he transfers the change which, partially through his own instrumentality, took place in the religious mind of his people, to the divine world itself. He makes use of the old, obscure legends of a struggle between the old gods and the new, in order to show us, in profound representations, how the awful law of the Eumenides gave place, in consequence, to a milder and more human system; how the original despotism of Zeus was transformed into a benevolent, moral rule of the world.

The fairest blossoming of this gentler spirit appears in the works of Sophocles. As no other poet brought classic art to such harmonious perfection, so there is no nobler representative of a pure religious faith, so far as this was possible on the ground of a Greek polytheism. With a feeling of the purest piety Sophocles delineates the gods, whose power and law encompass human life. All things come from them — the good and the evil; no mortal can withstand their never-changing power; no act nor thought can escape their all-seeing eye; none can venture to transgress their eternal laws. From the gods spring all wisdom; they guide us ever to the right. Their dispensations man may bear with resignation; he may commit all sorrow to Zeus; beyond the limits of man's nature he need not aspire. These propositions it is, and such as these, which cheer us so repeatedly in Sophocles, but which we also meet not rarely in other poets of that period. The bounds of Greek polytheism are by this certainly not transcended; yet still we must form another conception of the faith which expresses itself in this manner, than that which is commonly connected with the name of heathenism. The many gods are here, in the end, only the representatives of the one "Divine," or Deity. From their action in the world the caprice and conflict of which Homer is able to tell us so much has disappeared. There is one moral order of the world, which uses now one god, now another, as its instrument. The plurality of gods remains as the imagery of faith; but the discord which it threatened to create in the religious consciousness is in great part avoided.

It was also of great importance for the moral character of the religious convictions that, together with this development of the idea of God, the faith in a future recompense became stronger and more widely spread. In Homer and Hesiod only the barest beginnings of this doctrine are to be found. It first attained higher significance in the Eleusinian, but especially in the so-called Orphic, mysteries — a later branch of this form of worship, belonging seemingly, in its origin, to the sixth or seventh century B.C.; and in Pythagoreanism, which in the first place had its rise likewise from moral-religious, not from scientific, motives. The form, as well as the content, of this faith, whose history we cannot here follow further, was surely, in the first place, somewhat confused and cloudy; with the Orpheans and Pythagoreans it was joined with the mythical doctrine of the transmigration of souls; and that which was to decide future happiness or misery was, at least with the former, less moral worth or worthlessness than the relation to the secret services and to the asceticism bound up with them. He who had received initiation, who had kept himself from eating meat and the like, who had followed certain external rules of life, should in the future sit at table with the gods in the lower world; but the unconsecrated, on the contrary, should be cast into a slimy pool. But even by the Pythagoreans the belief in immortality was used in a more purely moral sense. In Pindar it contains the strongest moral incitements. Aeschylus's picture of the divine judgment concludes with the threat that even death does not free the criminal from the spirits of vengeance. Sophocles makes frequent reference to the recompense after death. And in Euripides we find the words: "Who knows whether, in truth, death be not life, but life death?" It is very clear how greatly the thought of the divine justice must needs win strength through this extension of its operations, and how much more actively the unity of the divine must have presented itself to consciousness when one and the same moral order embraced the living and the dead.

Greatly, however, as the older form of the Greek religion was thus ennobled, its polytheistic basis, as has been said, was not immediately touched by this development of the monotheistic element, which also lay in it. Another and a bolder course was taken by philosophy.

The Greek philosophy did not grow up, like the Christian, in the service of theology; its oldest representatives did not wish to defend or explain religious belief, but to investigate the nature of things. In so far they had no such immediate occasion to express themselves concerning the content of that belief as their Christian successors had. But since in their explanation of nature they fixed attention upon the world as a whole, in order to determine its ultimate grounds, they all proceeded expressly or tacitly from the presupposition of a unified, world-forming force, whether they thought of this as bound up with the material substance or separated from it — whether they designated it as Nature, or Deity, or in some other way. And several of them declared expressly that this force was to be sought only in the highest reason, only in the Infinite Spirit; most decidedly, and with the clearest scientific consciousness, among the pre-Socratic philosophers with whom we first have to do here, did Anaxagoras, the friend of the great Pericles, who lived in Athens until toward the end of the Peloponnesian war do this.

Towards the popular religion these men assume various attitudes, according to their own various characters. Many of them pursued the course of their scientific investigations, without defining their exact relation to the popular faith, and usually, indeed, without even settling the matter for themselves. Others leaned upon the popular representations so far as to use them for certain philosophical conceptions, treating the two as directly equivalent. And so it is naturally the form of Zeus, again, in which the ultimate ground of all things, the unity of the cosmical system, and of the forces working in the world are brought to view. Democritus makes the attempt to explain the gods themselves, along with the belief in the gods, from the presuppositions of his materialistic doctrine of nature : Through a concurrence of atoms, like that to which all else owes its existence, had risen also natures of superhuman form and greatness, whose appearance had called forth the belief in gods. And in like manner Empedocles causes the gods, " the long-living, the most honored," to be formed out of his four elements, like animals and men and all other things. To us, with our purer idea of God, these are most astonishing positions; but not so to the Greeks, in whose mythology, from the beginning, the generation of the various races of gods holds an important place, and among whom Pindar sings : " The race of men is one, the race of gods another ; but one mother gave birth to both." In this no attack was intended upon the popular faith.

Very decidedly, on the contrary, does this latter intention appear in the utterances of a man who belongs among the most remarkable phenomena in the history of the Greek consciousness — Xenophanes. This philosophical poet, the founder of the so-called Eleatic school, whose long life extends from the first decades of the sixth to beyond the beginning of the fifth century, was led, according to all advices, purely through his own reflection, to the most thorough-going doubts concerning the religion of his people. What impels him to this is not simply the likeness of gods to men, with their frequent excessive weaknesses, but also their multiplicity as such. Mortals believe, he says, that the gods are generated, as though it were not alike godless to speak of them as having become or as to die. And he expressed himself in the same sense, according to Aristotle, concerning the sacrifice and the lamentation for the sea-goddess, Leucothea : If men deem her mortal, they should not sacrifice to her ; if they deem her a divinity, they should not lament for her. The contradiction in the religion, in assuming a divinity, an infinite, and at the same time attributing to it finite conditions and properties, proves to the philosopher that this religion cannot be the true one. A similar contradiction, however, is pointed out by him in many other features of the Greek religion. As men think of the gods as having become, so they regard them as changeable. Motion in space is ascribed to them, when they are allowed to descend from heaven to earth, to visit this or that place of their worship, to appear here or there to render assistance, etc. It were not seemly for deity, he declares, to wander now here, now there; it can only remain unmoved in one place. Yet more strikingly in contradiction to his idea of the divine is the attribution to it of a human or of any outward form. Men lend the gods, he said, their own form, feeling, and voice, and each people lends them its own: the negroes think the gods black and flat-nosed; the Thracians think them blue-eyed and red-haired; and if the horses and oxen could paint, — he adds with bitter sarcasm, — they would, without doubt, represent them as horses and oxen. And it goes almost worse still with the gods in the depiction of their moral nature. "Hesiod and Homer attribute everything to the gods which redounds to the shame of men and calls forth censure — thievery, adultery, and mutual deception." But not alone these weaknesses and the likeness to men; the multiciplicity of gods as such is inconsistent, according to the purer insight of Xenophánes, with the conception of the divine nature. Deity, he shows, must be the most perfect; there can, however, be but one most perfect. Deity can only rule, it cannot be ruled; the existence, therefore, along with the highest, all-ruling God of other gods, subordinate to him, cannot be admitted. He is therefore himself able to think of but one God, who is high above all finite things. "One God," he sings, "among gods and among men," is the highest, not to be compared, in form or in thought, with mortals," — a God who, as it is said in another place, is all eye, all ear, all thought, who "rules all, untroubled, with the intelligence of his understanding." Thus monotheism here first appears with full consciousness, in fundamental opposition to the polytheism of the Greek popular faith and the humanization of the gods. From the conception of the divine nature were derived, through simple reasoning, the conclusions which could but shake to its centre the whole existing religion.

It must surely excite our deepest astonishment to find such pure and lofty conceptions of the divine, so clear a consciousness of that which the idea of God demands, in the midst of a polytheistic people, five hundred years before Christ, in a period in which scientific investigation had scarcely attempted its first uncertain steps. The historical effect of this phenomenon also we must not estimate too low. The attacks of Xenophanes inflicted a wound upon the Greek polytheism from which it never recovered; and if, indeed, this philosopher, with his bold doubts concerning the nature of the existing religion, stands for a time almost alone, he does not, on the one hand, entirely lack followers in the next fifty years; and further, those doubts grew up, in the end, to a power against which the popular religion had no means of resistance to oppose beyond the habit of the masses and isolated violent measures which were entirely without general effect.

A few decades after Xenophanes, we meet the Ephesian philosopher Heraclitus, — not exactly on the same way, to be sure, but still on a way that lies nearly enough to it. The plurality of gods is not, indeed, expressly attacked by him, far as he is above it, with his idea of the universal, all-directing reason; but the religious rites bound up so closely with the belief, the animal sacrifices and the image-worship, receive his decided censure; and concerning the poets whose works were for the Hellenes the most sacred religious sources, — concerning Homer and Hesiod, — he is unable to express himself strongly enough.

Somewhat later, about the middle of the fifth century, we

hear the thoughts, and indeed the very expressions, of the old Eleatic sound through a fragment of Empedocles, which speaks of Apollo, or indeed of the highest God, — for we do not know which, — " Him can man not approach, neither view with the eyes nor touch with the hands; for no human body and no limbs pertain to him, but he is a pure, holy, incomprehensible spirit, who with quick thoughts hastens through the universe." At the same time begins that *Aufklaerung* whose most outspoken representatives we are accustomed to designate as the Sophists — a movement which in a short time penetrated every department of Greek life and every grade of society, thoroughly shattered the traditional customs and convictions, and opened a vigorous attack from the inquiring upon the religious faith. We find the very first mouth-piece of the Sophists, Protagoras, beginning one of his works with the declaration that concerning the gods he has nothing to say, — neither that they exist nor that they do not exist, — for the subject is too dark, and human life is too short, for a thorough investigation. Another of the more famous Sophists, Prodicus, sought to show how men came to the belief in the gods through reverence for useful and beneficial natural objects; while Critias, a scholar of the Sophists, represented religion, in one of his dramas, as the invention of shrewd legislators, who wished to gain from the fear of divine retribution a support for the working of their laws. And this last was, indeed, in the circles to which the influence of the Sophistic *Aufklaerung* extended, the most current opinion. As in all other political institutions and customs, so also in religion, this school saw only the product of arbitrary agreement, and this the variety of religions seemed to them to prove. If the belief in the gods sprang from the nature of man, all men, according to their opinion, must worship the same gods; that it is precisely from the nature of the human mind and from the natural conditions of its development that the variety of religions, like that of all other historical forms of life, proceeds, — of this these Greek *Aufklaerers* had as little understanding as their modern successors.

But however superficially they might proceed in this connection, the spirit of the time came so strongly to their assistance in the intellectually most important Greek cities, and their way of thinking was so little confined to the schools, that about the time of the Peloponnesian war, — and not in Athens alone,— it is to be looked upon as the prevailing view among the educated classes.

That which the Sophists delivered in their writings and pompous speeches, the poets preached in another form, with the most important and general effect, from the theatre. While a Sophocles raised, in his tragedies, a monument no less of his pious feeling than of his art, we find his younger contemporary, Euripides, the scholar of Anaxagoras, mixing with many fine religious and moral passages a mass of doubts on dogmatic and moral points. We meet in him such a naturalistic treatment of the myths that it becomes undeniably apparent how far removed he is from the stand-point of the old religion. The comedian Aristophanes rails with passionate vehemence against him and against all the *moderns*, among whom he even reckons Socrates. And we cannot doubt that, with his zeal for the old customs and the old faith, he was in his way earnest. But is it to be called restoring the reverence for the gods, when one sacrifices them with such wild wantonness as Aristophanes to the laughter of the spectators; when one uncovers the nakedness of their humanness so glaringly and roughly as he; when one draws them so far into all the smut of the low and vulgar? And that this part of his pieces found far more sympathy among his hearers than the exhortations to a return to the good old time and its faith, — that, even in the first decade of the Peloponnesian war, it was accounted by very many in Athens as decidedly unrefined and old-fashioned to still believe in the gods, he tells us himself. If even his pious, and often so superstitious, older contemporary, Herodotus, holds himself by no means free from the influences of the rationalistic *Aufklaerung*, we see in a Thucydides how, toward the end of the fifth century, the deepest earnestness of feeling, the sublimest moral contemplation of the world, could exist along with an utter absence of that mythical element which is so indispensable to the old Greek religion; yet even this historian sets before our eyes in striking pictures the confusion of all moral ideas, the disappearance of piety and faith, the prevalence, during the internal struggles of the Greek states, of a bald selfishness.

The Sophists, with their attacks on the popular faith, are only the foremost champions of a way of thinking which, prepared for in that time from the most various sides, is not to be regarded as the work of these individuals, but only as the product of the entire historical development. So much the less was it to be expected that isolated interferences of political power, — prosecutions such as were instituted even in the lifetime of Pericles, by the political opponents of that statesman, against Anaxagoras, and later against Protagoras and Socrates, — would oppose a lasting barrier to the innovations. Certain individuals fell victims to these charges. Anaxagoras and Protagoras were forced to leave Athens; Socrates drank the hemlock; but the diffusion of the views of these men was not checked, but promoted, by persecution. When Protagoras fled from Athens, about the year 410 B.C., the unbelief which was persecuted in him had long shot forth in that city the deepest and most wide-spreading roots. A restoration of the popular religion in its former import had already become an impossibility; but beyond the standpoint of the Sophists it was certainly possible to advance, when deeper spirits and profounder thinkers took up the task which the Sophists had handled one-sidedly and unsatisfyingly.

Such a profounder thinker was Socrates. This great philosopher endeavored, indeed, on principle, to abstain from all theological investigations. The human reason, he believed, is not in a position to fathom the nature and the works of Deity, and this research also has no use; and he censured the natural philosophers for thinking that they could come upon the traces of the workings of the gods. He wished, for his part, to limit himself to the things which concern human life and human duties. But since he reckoned among these duties, before all else, piety and reverence towards the gods, he was compelled to form a definite opinion concerning Deity and its relation to man; and since he could naturally proceed in this only in accordance with his general principles, he became, almost against his will, the author of a theology, which, in spite of its scientific deficiencies, became of great importance for the following time. As he was accustomed to estimate the worth of human actions according to the reasonableness of their purposes, so he sought also in the universe, in the first place, for the purpose which everything has to serve; this he is to be believed to recognize in the welfare of man. He came thus to the conviction that the world can only be the work of an almighty, all-gracious, all-wise, all-knowing Being; a Being whose reason as far transcends ours as the greatness of the world in which it is inherent exceeds the greatness of our body; whose eye penetrates all; whose care embraces all, the greatest and the smallest alike. Socrates had in this no need to inquire more closely into the relation of this rational faith of his to the popular religion, to which he was uprightly attached. He speaks, according to the manner of the Greeks, without distinction, now in the plural of the gods, now in the singular of God or the Divine; he is convinced that the gods rule all things for our best, that we have to resign ourselves unconditionally to their dispensations, unconditionally to obey their commands; and as to the worship of the gods, he quiets himself with the remark that a pious disposition is the best religious service; that, for the rest, each may worship the Deity according to the custom of his people. Still, it is not to be denied that his religious faith proceeds, in the main, from the unity of the divine. He does not deny the many gods of the popular religion; much rather, he believed in them, without doubt, in all earnestness; but above these many gods rises the one world-forming reason so decidedly, as the essential, as that which for the ordering of the world and the moral work of man is alone decisive, that they appear beside it almost as useless additions.

Socrates himself, in a declaration which Xenophon has given us, distinguishes thus between the two, when he says that the other gods, as well as the Former and Preserver of the universe, evince their kindness to us, without revealing themselves to our gaze. The main point for him lies in the conviction that everything in the world and in human life is ordered according to the best purposes, with perfect reason, according to a unified plan; whether there be only one Being from whom this order proceeds, or whether there be under the highest Deity other divine beings who serve as assistants, is a question whose investigation troubles him little, because it seems to him to be of no consequence for his practical religious needs. For his own part, however, he could but be inclined to give preference to the second postulate, for the reason that it best agreed with the faith of his people, from which he held it to be neither necessary nor permissible to separate himself. The unity of God is thus connected with the plurality of the popular gods in the way which had been approximated through the mythology, and in which the poets had already taken the lead of the philosophers; the many gods are placed in a thoroughly subordinate relation to the One; they have only to represent, in the separate portions of the world and in the various relations of human life, that reason which is viewed as universal, the power embracing the universe, in the highest sense God.

To this course Greek philosophy, in the great majority of its representatives, remained true. There were, indeed, certainly not lacking among them those who assumed a bolder attitude towards the popular religion. If Socrates had distinguished the highest God from the remaining gods, his scholar, Antisthenes, declared, with the Eleatics, that there is in truth only one God, whom we may not represent to ourselves in human form; popular opinion alone had created the many gods. And he himself, as well as his followers, the Cynics, distinguished themselves by a free-thinking which we also find again later among the Cynics of the Roman imperial period, while they sought to use the mythical traditions for moral purposes by a free allegorical exposition. Another Socratic, Aristippus, who also strayed far in other respects from the genuine Socratic doctrine, followed with his school the sceptical views of Protagoras.

Of the later schools of the Alexandrian and Roman periods, the Sceptics and Epicureans are those who opposed themselves as *Aufklaerers* to the popular religion. The first could not, indeed, logically raise positive objections to the existence of the gods; but they declared it to be incapable of proof, like every other scientific proposition; and Carneades especially, the most acute of the old Sceptics, in the second century before Christ, raised objections against the common conception of God, in the controversy with the theology of the contemporaneous Stoical school, which have not even yet entirely lost their significance. The numerous school of the Epicureans, which extended itself especially among the Romans, withdrew from the popular faith on another side. These philosophers had no desire to question the existence of the gods; they declared this much rather to be quite incontrovertible. But, in order that the principle of a purely physical explanation of nature might not be at all prejudiced, and in order to cut away the roots of the superstitious fear of Deity, they held it to be necessary to explain away every influence of the gods upon earthly things. The gods were said to dwell in blessed rest, as objects of a disinterested reverence, in the empty spaces between the worlds, untouched by our affairs, and not intrenching upon them; whereas within the worlds everything was said to be governed partly by accident, partly by blind natural necessity.

From this belief, which was scarcely distinguished in its practical effects from atheism, monotheism had nothing to hope. The Epicureans opposed it with the same mockery as the myths of the popular religion; and just as little could the doubts of the Sceptics concerning the popular conceptions advance a purer faith, since they held the existence of one

God and the existence of many gods to be equally indemonstrable. These schools, therefore, promoted the cause of monotheism only mediately, so far as they contributed, by breaking to pieces the existing religion, to pave the way for a new.

This way of thinking, however, as has been remarked, did not have the mastery in Greek philosophy. The most important of the post-Socratic philosophers followed much rather the course, which Socrates had already chosen, of reconciling polytheism with monotheism. Yet, at the same time, they went beyond Socrates, through opposing themselves much more freely than he to the popular religion, and insisting much more distinctly upon its purification through philosophy. In this connection, however, no other exercised so profound an influence upon the development of the religious consciousness — an influence extending itself over many centuries — as the great scholar of Socrates, Plato. This philosopher's religious view or *Welt-anschauung* is, in its fundamental determinations, a highly pure and spiritual monotheism. Above and behind the phenomenal world there lies, according to him, the world of eternal, immaterial, unchangeable essences — the *ideas;* and at the head of the united world of ideas stands the *good*, the infinite essence, which is the ground of all thought and all being, which gives to all things their reality and to our conceptions their truth, towards which all our thoughts and activities in their innermost nature tend, — if, indeed, we are able to behold it only with difficulty in its pure form, and, for the most part, only in its images and effects. From the good Plato's world-forming Deity does not substantially differ, and it is the idea of the good by which his conception of Deity is everywhere penetrated and determined. Goodness is the most essential attribute of Deity; out of goodness it has formed the world; with goodness and wisdom it directs human destiny, in the small as in the great. He who imitates, by purity of life, its goodness and perfection must in the end be served by all things for the best. By the idea of the good are our conceptions of Deity to be measured; according to it, are our duties to Deity to be judged. The Deity is not jealous of human happiness, as the popular belief in fate imagined; for the good is without envy. It cannot change itself, and cannot show itself other than it is, because the perfect is unchangeable, and all untruth is foreign to it. It must be throughout a spiritual nature, high above liking and dislike, untouched by every evil; of its power, its goodness, its wisdom, its holiness, its justice, we may form only the loftiest and purest conceptions; the myths, which ascribe human weaknesses, passions, and mistakes to the gods, we must oppose as unworthy fables. True worship also can consist only in pure feeling and virtuous life, not in prayers and gifts, with which unreasonableness hopes to honor the gods and baseness hopes to bribe them.

We must admit that these are principles than which purer can scarcely be found, even on Christian ground; and, indeed, these Platonic apothegms have served the teachers of the Christian church for centuries as a rule for their representations of the Deity and for their comprehension of biblical narrations. A philosopher who held such views had essentially outgrown Greek polytheism. None the less, however, Plato will not abandon it unconditionally. And even his system offered him certainly a few points of connection. On the one hand, there stand under and alongside the Deity, or the good, the other ideas, which he also indeed designates as the eternal gods; on the other hand, Plato could not forsake the popular view, according to which the constellations, in the unchanging regularity of their course, were accounted living beings, in which a far higher reason was immanent than in man; and he likewise holds the universe to be a living being, from whose soul are derived the souls of all individuals. The constellations are therefore, as he says, the visible gods, and he calls the world the god that has become, whose beauty and perfection he cannot sufficiently praise. The remaining gods of the Greek popular faith, on the contrary,—an Apollo, a Here, an

Athene, etc., — he considers, as he unambiguously gives us to understand, as mythical forms. But even these he will not have removed, on that account, from the public religious worship, and he will have the belief in them made the foundation of public education; for men, he says, must in the first place be educated through untruths, afterwards through the truth — first through myths, then through scientific knowledge. He, therefore, who does not arrive at the latter — and this is the case with the mass of men — remains throughout life relegated to the myths and the form of worship corresponding to them. Only so much the more earnestly does the philosopher urge that the myths themselves be purified, from moral and philosophical points of view — that everything morally detrimental and unworthy of the divine be removed from the religious tradition and from the worship; and precisely here lies the main ground of the severity of his judgments upon the great poets of his people, and the strictness with which he refuses a Homer and a Hesiod admittance to his state. As poets, he would perhaps tolerate them; as teachers of religion, he must reject them.

Everything taken together, his position in relation to our question is consequently this: He is himself a monotheist, and this monotheism scarcely suffers a limitation through the doctrine of the higher nature of the constellations; for these visible gods stand essentially in similar relation to the one invisible God as man or any other of the finite beings. As a religion for the people, on the contrary, he deems the Hellenic polytheism indispensable; but he demands as the condition of its admissibility that it be subjected to a thorough reform, and be brought by this, as far as possible, into harmony with that monotheism in its workings.

Aristotle is at one with Plato in all main points. The doctrine of the unity of God is still more distinctly expressed by him than by Plato. As the world is only one, he points out, it must also be moved by one highest cause; and this cause, as he further deduces, can only be extramundane, pure spirit, working in uninterrupted, never-slumbering activity of thought. At the same time, the determination that the Deity must be a personal Being comes out more expressly in him than in Plato, and is more deeply grounded in his entire system. The Socratic-Platonic belief in providence, on the contrary, is essentially limited. The Deity is, indeed, according to Aristotle, the first moving cause, which gives impetus to the revolution of the heaven, and the highest good, to which all tends. There rules, indeed, in nature, a universal activity, working unconsciously from within according to a purpose, and in human life a natural connection of moral worth with inward happiness; but for an immediate intrenchment of Deity upon the course of the world, extending to particulars, there is no place in the Aristotelian system. Alongside the highest God Aristotle also accepts a number of other eternal beings, in the spirits of the heavenly spheres, as he also declares the universe to be without beginning and imperishable, since the divine activity in the world must be even as eternal as Deity itself. To these spirits of the stars he also refers the polytheistic faith, so far as he concedes it any truth. "All things remaining, however," he says, "are mythical additions for winning the masses, made for the sake of legislation and common needs." We have therefore here, likewise, a monotheism which is but little modified by the acceptance of spirits of the stars, and which is chiefly distinguished from the Platonic only by a severer, less imaginative character — a monotheism which has for itself no need of the popular religion, but which still tolerates it as a political necessity, and leaves open for it certain points of connection in its own system.

In the next great Greek school of philosophy, the Stoic, this monotheism becomes pantheism. One Being there is, according to the Stoical teaching, from which proceed the matter and the form of all things, and which at the end of this world-period will take all back into itself, in order, after the expiration of a fixed time, to create the same world anew, and to continue to all eternity the succession of things, as it has endured from eternity. This Being is at the same time the primitive substance and the primitive force; it is the creative fire, which in its transformation produces the remaining elements; but it is also the highest spirit, the reason and the law of the world, the Deity. Everything which exists has become from this Divine Being, and is sustained by it. All natural forces and all spirits are only portions of the one force which pours itself through all. So far now as a divine force works in everything, everything can be made an object of religious worship, be personified as a Deity; but since in truth it is only one force, which appears under different forms in all things, these divine forms may not be treated as independent personal beings, but only as mythical representations of natural forces, which, having risen from the one source of the divine nature, stream in a thousand branches through the universe. From this double point of view is the conception of religion determined in the Stoical school. On the one hand, they oppose to Scepticism and Epicureanism the substance of the popular faith; they seek to show that the representations of the gods and the myths, which are indeed apparently most unworthy and unreasonable, have their good sense; they endeavor to defend the belief in prophecy and similar things. On the other hand, however, they cannot sanction all this in the same sense which it had in the faith of the people. In place of the gods appear natural things — the stars, the elements, the fruits of the earth, great men, and the benefactors of mankind; in place of the immediate divine revelations appear the natural foretokens of future events, which the wise and experienced can recognize and explain by means of the connection and consistency of all things. Their treatment of the popular religion is therefore a continual explaining around the same; they are the chief authors of that allegorical mode of interpretation which passed from the Greeks to the Jews, and on to the Christians, and has created with both so much confusion. A pantheistic monotheism seeks here to come to terms with polytheism by artificial means. But that the two are none the less of different nature is not entirely hidden even among the Stoics. From them, also, we receive not only many fine passages concerning the Deity, the worthlessness of a merely outward service, and the necessity of a spiritual worship, but also very sharp and free judgments concerning the myths and the public worship; but the school as a whole had too little critical sense to become perfectly clear as to its relation to the popular religion.

In Plato, Aristotle, and the Stoics we have become acquainted with the three main sources of the religious views to which for many centuries, in the Graeco-Roman and the Graeco-Oriental world, all those held to whom the popular religion was too crude and dull, irreligion too comfortless and void. In the eclecticism of the Roman period the doctrines of these men were mixed in the most various combinations. At the same time, however, even among the philosophers, the disposition became more and more extended to lean upon the positive religion, and to expect from divine revelation the communication of truth, as to the independent discovery of which the weary thought had already, since the appearance of Scepticism, begun to despair. And the further Deity was removed above everything finite and earthly, by the purer idea of God in the Platonic and Aristotelian school, the more forcibly was the need felt of finding a mediation between the two in such natures as should be higher than man, but at the same time should stand nearer to the world and man than Deity. Hence the importance now won by the belief in demons. This belief had been formerly only a subordinate element of the popular religion — was, indeed, made use of occasionally by the philosophers, as by Plato, but remained foreign to their own convictions. It now became a subject of the most earnest religious interest. Of the one God of the philosophers there existed too high conceptions to allow of the venture to weave him, with his activity and his essence, into the course of nature and human affairs. The gods of the people, who were said to be woven into both, it was impossible, for that very reason, to treat as gods in the strict and full sense. But the need which polytheism had begotten was not yet removed; the habit of bringing the divine to view in sensible presence and defined appearance could not be broken. What else remained but to place a number of subordinate beings beside the Deity, who should constitute the bond between it and the world; since they carried the divine forces over into the finite, and took the particular parts of the world and individual men under their special protection? These beings are the demons. They are the old gods of polytheism, but stripped of their independent lordship, subordinated to the one monotheistic God, as his servants and instruments. Since the demons take the place of the gods for the religious consciousness, polytheism declares itself ready to subject itself to monotheism, in case the latter is disposed to vouchsafe it at least a subordinate place within itself.

This disposition was just then widespread in the sole strictly monotheistic religion of antiquity — Judaism. In the centuries immediately succeeding the Babylonish captivity a new element had penetrated into the circle of Jewish conceptions, in the belief in angels and devils, which offered the polytheistic mode of thought a certain satisfaction inside of monotheism. Between the old gods, who had subjected themselves as demons and lower divinities to a higher god, and the ministering spirits who now surrounded the one God of Judaism, the difference was so slight that nothing essential seemed to stand in the way of a blending together of the two. And, indeed, the Jewish Alexandrians began already to set forth a theory concerning the divine forces, and concerning the bearer of all these forces, the Logos or Word of God, in which the Jewish belief in angels entered into the closest union with the Greek belief in demons, and with the philosophers' doctrines of the ideas and the universal, all-penetrating divine reason (the divine Logos).

But preparation for this blending of the religions was also made from yet another side. Partly by the mixing of peoples in the Alexandrian and Roman time, partly by the Greek philosophy, the barriers were broken through, which until then held the nations separated from one another in self-sufficient exclusiveness. The Hellene had to accustom himself to acknowledge also among the barbarians the moral and spiritual qualities, on the presumed sole possession of which his proud contempt of everything not Greek had hitherto propped itself. The Jew was constrained to doubt the exclusive choice of his people, after he met among the Greeks a surpassing spiritual culture, which was also a gift of God, and an insight in religious things, with the acknowledgment of which his national vanity contented itself, sorrowfully enough, through the groundless pretence that the old wise men of Greece had borrowed their treasures from the Jewish prophets and the Old Testament writings. Thus the knowledge gradually broke in — the lasting extension of which is to be ascribed before all to the Stoical school, to its immortal merit — that all men, by reason of their rational character, are of the same nature and stand under the same law; that they have the same natural rights and the same moral duties; that they are all equally to be considered as children of God, as citizens of one and the same commonwealth, which embraces all mankind. Men learned to conceive the relation of man to God as an immediate and inner one, to view the service of the devout heart and the virtuous life as more essential than the national form of worship, to dispense with priestly mediation for the communion of man with God. This purification of the morally religious consciousness was first perfected in comprehensive manner among the Greeks and through the Greek philosophy; but even Judaism had not shut herself up from it; and since the second century before Christ a party had appeared here, in the Essenes, which, in undeniable connection with the Greek new Pythagoreanism, and through this with the collective philosophy of that time, devoted itself to an inner, solitary piety, directed to poverty and renunciation, to universal philanthropy and the removal of all inequality among men; was indifferent, on the contrary, to the national Messianic hopes, rejected the entire principle of sacrifices, — the central point of the Jewish religious service,

— and opposed to the hierarchical institutions of Judaism a monastically organized union of ascetics.

This change in the moral consciousness, however, stands in the closest connection with the development of the conceptions of Deity. When, in place of the many gods, there appeared the one God whose kingdom is the entire world, it became necessary also that one divine right and law should embrace all men; consequently not only did national particularism have to fall, but also the universal service of the devout life appeared as the essential, in opposition to particular and external rituals. Even so, *vice versa*, when the consciousness of the brotherhood and equality of all men was arrived at, it was impossible to hold fast to the diversity of gods; if mankind is but one, — if it has one end and stands under one law, — it can be only one and the same power by which all men are created and ruled. The belief in the unity of God and the belief in the equality of all men and their moral duties condition each other reciprocally; both developed together in the old world, and thus prepared for Christianity the ground in which it could not plant the germ of a new religion and a new moral life, as it were, from without, but out of which alone it could itself grow and draw its nourishment according to the laws of historical development.

But, important as the place is which Greek philosophy fills among the forces which prepared the way for Christianity,— when this itself appeared in its distinctness, and declared war upon the polytheistic popular religions of the earlier time, then it was precisely this philosophy which became the last champion of paganism. We certainly cannot say this without limitation. Not a few philosophically educated men went over to the new religion; very many more acquired, as Christians, in the schools of the philosophers the scientific culture which they needed for the defence and the theological formulation of their faith. The Hellenic philosophy thus worked not only outside the church and against the church, but also in it and for it. And a more careful investigation would show that its influence on the Christian theology and

Christian usage was from the beginning incomparably more extensive and permanent than is generally conceived. But the majority of the Greek philosophers regarded a faith which appeared to them in the positive part of its creed as superstition, and in its attack upon the existing religions as mischievous, with profound contempt; and as this faith grew into a threatening, and finally conquering power, they opposed it with bitter hatred.

About the middle of the third century Greek philosophy gathered together, for the last time, in the Neo-Platonic school, all the forces which yet remained to it. The doctrinal system of this school appears, in its theological content, as an acute, accomplished attempt to unite the philosophical monotheism with that polytheism from which the Hellenic feeling cut itself loose with so great difficulty. The mode of union is nearly related to that which we have already noticed in the Stoical teaching, if, indeed, the more particular determinations have a different purport. One Supreme Being is assumed, indeterminable, incomprehensible, inconceivable, but at the same time the source of all existence and the seat of all perfection. By him proceeds, by an overflowing of his fulness, by a naturally necessary working of his power, the gradation of the finite; but the farther things are removed from their source, the more mediums lie between the two, the more imperfect they become, till in the end the pure light of the divine forces goes out in the darkness of matter. All things consequently form a gradual succession, of diminishing perfection. All are sustained by divine forces; but these are apportioned to them in different measure and different purity. For this very reason, however, say the New-Platonists, is it necessary that we press upward from the lower stages, through the intermediate, to the higher; that we allow ourselves to be led, in regular ascent, from the lower gods to the highest God; that we despise not the sensuous mediums of spiritual goods. And since they explain the Greek and Oriental divinities, with all the arbitrariness of the established allegorical exposition, into the abstract categories of their metaphysics; since they seek the natural medium of a higher life not in the knowledge and cultivation of the real, but in the ritualistic proceedings of all the popular religions and mysteries, in sacrifices and prayers, prophecy and consecration, image-worship and theurgy, everything rude and fantastic out of the mythology, all the externalities of worship, all the varied superstition of thousands of years find in their system an artificial justification. Against the purer doctrine and moral force of Christianity this system could not long hold its ground; but so great was the underlying power of the Greek spirit, which had become wearied and in so many respects untrue to itself, that the victorious church, even during the conflict, took up into itself the same philosophy which had made the Hellenic ground so hard to conquer. New-Platonism was conquered, so far as it had identified itself with paganism; as a form of Christian speculation, the church itself appropriated it. To the writings which a Christian New-Platonist, about the year 500, fathered upon Dionysius the Areopagite the church paid the highest reverence. The church defended its dogmas, its sacraments, its hierarchical institutions with the same principles which it had had before to fight in its pagan opponents. On this side, indeed, the influence of the Greek nature may be traced up to the present. Far more important, however, certainly, is the service which Greek science rendered to all after time in the opposite direction, through the refining of religious ideas and the purification of moral conceptions. And of this service I trust that I have given, in the narrow bounds prescribed me, a not altogether unsatisfactory representation

ARTICLE III.

THE TRIAL OF CHRIST:[1] A DIATESSARON WITH DISSERTATIONS.

BY HENRY C. VEDDER, OF THE EXAMINER'S EDITORIAL STAFF, NEW YORK.

DIATESSARON.[2]

AND immediately, while he is still speaking, cometh Judas Iscariot, one of the twelve, and with him a great multitude with swords and staves, and with lanterns and torches, having received the band and officers from the chief priests and scribes and pharisees and elders of the people. Then the band and the captain and the officers of the Jews took Jesus and bound him.
<small>Matt. xxvi. 47.
Mark xiv. 43.
Luke xxii. 47.
John xviii. 3,12.</small>

And they led him to Annas first, for he was father-in-law to Caiaphas, who was high-priest that year. Now Caiaphas was he who gave counsel to the Jews that it was expedient that one man should die for the people.
<small>John xviii. 13,14.</small>

And they that had laid hold of Jesus led him away to Caiaphas, the high-priest, where the chief priests and the scribes and the elders assembled. The high-priest then asked Jesus of his disciples and of his doctrine. Jesus answered him: I have spoken openly to the world; I ever taught in the synagogue and in the temple, whither all the Jews resort; and in secret have I said nothing. Why askest thou me? Ask them who heard me what I have said unto them. Behold! they know what I said. And when he had thus spoken, one of the officers who stood by smote Jesus with the palm of his hand, saying, Answerest thou the high-priest so? Jesus answered him: If I have spoken evil, bear witness of the evil; but if well, why smitest thou me? Now Annas had sent him bound unto Caiaphas, the high-priest.
<small>Matt. xxvi. 57.
Mark xiv. 53.
Luke xxii. 54.
John xviii. 19-24.</small>

Now the chief priests and the whole Sanhedrim kept seeking[3] for false witness against Jesus, in order to put him to death, and found none.

---

[1] A brief section recording the *arrest* of Jesus is prefixed to the account of the trial. The reason will appear in the sequel.

[2] The translation is that of the A. V., changes being made only when greater faithfulness to the Greek demanded them. The Greek text followed is that of Tischendorf's eighth edition.

[3] ἐζήτουν.

For many kept testifying falsely[1] against him, yet their testimony agreed not. At last there came two and bare false witness against him, saying: We heard this fellow say, I will destroy this temple of God, that is made with hands, and within three days I will build another made without hands. But neither so did their witness agree. And the high-priest stood up in the midst and asked Jesus, saying: Answerest thou nothing? What witness these against thee? But Jesus held his peace and answered nothing. And again the high-priest asked him, saying, I adjure thee by the living God, that thou tell us if thou be the Christ, the Son of God! Jesus saith unto him: Thou hast said. Moreover, I say unto you, hereafter shall ye see the Son of Man sitting on the right hand of power, and coming upon the clouds of heaven. Then the high-priest rent his clothes, saying: He hath spoken blasphemy! What further need have we of witnesses? Behold! now have ye heard his blasphemy. What think ye? And they all condemned him, saying, He is guilty of death.   *Matt. xxvi. 59-66. Mark xiv. 55-64.*

And the men that held him mocked him; and some began to spit in his face and to blindfold him, and to buffet him, and to say unto him: Prophecy unto us, thou Christ, Who is he that smote thee. And many other things blasphemously spake they against him. And the servants did strike him with the palms of their hands.   *Matt. xxvi. 67, 68. Mark xiv. 65, 66. Luke xxii. 63-65.*

And straightway in the morning, as soon as it was day, all the chief priests held a consultation with the elders and the scribes and the whole Sanhedrim, and took counsel against Jesus, to put him to death. And they led him away[2] into the Sanhedrim, saying, If thou art the Christ tell us. And he said unto them: If I tell you ye will not believe; and if I ask you ye will not answer. Hereafter the Son of Man shall be sitting on the right hand of the power of God. Then said they all, Art thou then the Son of God? And he said to them, Ye say that I am. And they said, What further need of testimony have we? For we ourselves have heard from his own mouth.   *Mark xv. 1. Luke xxii. 67-71.*

And the whole Sanhedrim rose up, and having bound Jesus led him away from Caiaphas to the *pretorium*, and delivered him to Pilate, the governor. And it was early. And they themselves went not into the judgment-hall, lest they should be defiled; but that they might eat the passover. Pilate therefore went out unto them, and saith, What accusation bring ye against this man? They answered and said, If he were not a malefactor we would not have delivered him up to thee. Then said Pilate unto them, Take ye him and judge according to your law. The Jews, therefore, said unto him, It is   *Matt. xxvii. 2. Mark xv. 1. Luke xxiii. 1. John xviii 28.*   *John xviii. 29-32.*

---

[1] ἐψευδομαρτύρουν.   [2] ἀπήγαγον, Luke xxii. 66.

not lawful for us to put any man to death: that the saying of Jesus might be fulfilled, which he spake signifying what death he should die. And they began to accuse him, saying: We found this fellow perverting our nation, and forbidding to give tribute to Caesar, and saying that he himself is Christ, a king.

<small>Luke xxiii. 2.</small>

Then Pilate entered into the judgment-hall again, and called Jesus. And Jesus stood before the governor, and the governor asked him, saying, Art thou the King of the Jews? Jesus answered, Of thyself sayest thou this, or did others tell it thee of me? Pilate answered: Am I a Jew? Thine own nation and the chief priests have delivered thee unto me; what hast thou done? Jesus answered: My kingdom is not of this world. If my kingdom were of this world, then would my servants be fighting that I should not be delivered to the Jews; but now is my kingdom not from hence. Pilate therefore said unto him, Art thou a king, then? Jesus answered: Thou sayest that I am a king. To this end was I born, and for this cause came I into the world, that I should bear witness unto the truth. Every one that is of the truth heareth my voice. Pilate saith unto him, What is truth? And when he had said this he went out again unto the Jews.

<small>John xviii. 33-38.</small>

And the chief priests and elders accused him of many things, but he answered nothing. Then said Pilate unto him: Answerest thou nothing? Hearest thou not how many things they witness against thee? But Jesus yet answered him never a word, insomuch that the governor marvelled greatly. Then said Pilate to the chief priests and to the people: I find no fault in this man. And they were the more fierce, saying: He stirreth up the people, teaching throughout all Jewry, beginning from Galilee to this place.

<small>Matt. xxvii. 12-14.
Mark xv. 3-5.</small>

<small>Luke xxiii. 4, 5.
John xviii. 38.</small>

When Pilate heard, he asked if the man were a Galilean. And as soon as he heard that he belonged to Herod's jurisdiction, he sent him to Herod, who himself was also at Jerusalem at that time. And when Herod saw Jesus he was exceeding glad, for he had been for a long season desirous to see him, because he had heard of him, and was hoping to see some miracle done by him. Then he questioned with him in many words, but he answered him nothing. And the chief priests and the scribes stood accusing him vehemently. And Herod with his men of war set him at naught and mocked him, and arrayed him in a gorgeous robe and sent him again to Pilate. And the same day Herod and Pilate were made friends together, for before they were at enmity between themselves. And Pilate, when he had called together the chief priests and the rulers and the people, said unto them: Ye have brought this man unto me as one that perverteth the people; and behold! I, having examined him before you, have found no fault in this man touching those things whereof ye accuse

<small>Luke xxiii. 6-12.</small>

<small>Luke xxiii. 13-16.</small>

him — no nor yet Herod, for he sent him to us; and lo! nothing worthy of death is done unto him. I will therefore chastise him and release him.

Now at the feast the governor was wont to release unto the people a prisoner, whom they would. And they had then a notable prisoner, named Barabbas, bound with them that had made insurrection with him, who had committed murder in the insurrection. And the multitude coming up began to desire him to do as he was wont to do unto them. Therefore, when they were gathered together, Pilate said unto them, Whom will ye that I release unto you, Barabbas or Jesus, the King of the Jews, who is called Christ? (For he knew that for envy they had delivered him.) But the chief priests and elders persuaded the multitude that they should ask Barabbas and destroy Jesus. And Pilate answered and said again unto them, Whether of the twain will ye that I release unto you? And they cried out all at once, saying, Away with this man, and release unto us Barabbas. Pilate, therefore, willing to release Jesus, spake again to them: What shall I do then with Jesus who is called Christ, whom ye call the King of the Jews? And they cried out again, Crucify him, crucify him. Then Pilate said unto them the third time: Why, what evil hath he done? I have found no cause of death in him. I will therefore chastise him and let him go. And they were instant with loud voices, crying out the more exceedingly, Crucify him. *Matt. xxvii. 15-23. Mark xv. 6-14. Luke xxiii. 19-23. John xviii. 39, 40.*

Pilate, seeing that he can prevail nothing, but rather a tumult is made, took water and washed his hands before the multitude, saying, I am innocent of this blood, see ye to it. Then answered all the people and said, His blood be upon us and upon our children. And Pilate wishing to content the people, released unto them him that for sedition and murder was cast into prison, whom they had desired; but Jesus he delivered to their will. Then Pilate therefore took Jesus and scourged him. Then the soldiers of the governor took Jesus into the common hall, called *pretorium*, and gathered unto him the whole band. And they stripped him and put on him a scarlet robe. And when they had platted a crown of thorns they put it upon his head, and a reed in his right hand. And bowing the knee before him they did homage to him and mocked him, saying, Hail, King of the Jews! And they spat upon him, and smote him with their hands, and took the reed and smote him on the head. *Matt. xxvii. 24-26. Mark xv. 15-19. Luke xxiii. 24, 25. John xix. 1-3.*

Pilate therefore went forth again, and said unto them, Behold! I bring him forth unto you that ye may know I find no fault in him. Then came Jesus forth, wearing the crown of thorns and the purple robe. And Pilate saith unto them, Behold the man! When the chief priests therefore and officers saw him, they cried out, saying, Crucify him, crucify him. Pilate saith unto them, Take ye him and crucify him, for I find no fault in him. The Jews answered him, We have a law, and by that law he ought to die, because he made himself the Son of God. When Pilate therefore heard that saying he was the more afraid and went again unto the judgment-hall, and saith unto Jesus, Whence art thou? But Jesus gave him no answer. Then saith Pilate unto him: Speakest thou not unto me? Knowest thou not that I have power to crucify thee, and have power to release thee? Jesus answered: Thou hast no power at all against me, except it were given thee from above; therefore he that delivered me unto thee hath the greater sin. And from thenceforth Pilate sought to release him, but the Jews cried out, saying: If thou let this man go, thou art not Caesar's friend. Whosoever maketh himself king speaketh against Caesar.

John xix. 4-12.

When Pilate therefore heard these words, he brought Jesus forth and sat down upon the bema,[1] in a place that is called the Pavement, but in the Hebrew *Gabbatha*. When he was set down upon the bema, his wife sent unto him, saying: Have thou nothing to do with that just man; for I have suffered many things this day in a dream because of him. And it was the preparation of the passover, about the sixth hour; and he saith unto the Jews, Behold your King! They therefore cried out, Away, away, crucify him! Pilate saith unto them, Shall I crucify your King? The chief priests answered, We have no king but Caesar. Then delivered he him, therefore, unto them to be crucified.

John xix. 13.

Matt. xxvii. 19.

John xix. 14-16.
Mark xv. 20.

DISSERTATION I.—CHRONOLOGY OF THE TRIAL.

To fix the exact order of the events narrated by the evangelists is not the easiest of tasks. The difficulty will be more apparent if the several accounts, briefly summarized, are placed in parallel columns:

MATTHEW.	MARK.	LUKE.	JOHN.
Jesus is led to "the high-priest," Caiaphas.	Jesus is led to "the high-priest." The Sanhedrim assembles. Jesus is tried, convicted, and insulted. In the morning the Sanhedrim reassembles and leads Jesus to Pilate.	Jesus is led to "the high-priest's palace," where he is mocked. At daybreak the Sanhedrim assembles, and Jesus is led away to it. He is tried, convicted, and at once led to Pilate.	Jesus is led to Annas first. "The high-priest" examines him. He is led from Caiaphas to the *prætorium* of Pilate.

This certainly looks discouraging. Sceptical critics declare

---

[1] ἐπὶ βήματος, in the judgment-seat. — A. V.

that these conflicting accounts cannot possibly be harmonized. On closer examination, however, many of the difficulties vanish. None of the writers pretends to give a complete account of the trial, but each one gives such items as especially impressed themselves upon his mind. Two questions only are at all difficult of solution: Where did the examination by the high-priest described by Luke take place? and, Does Luke describe the same trial as that recorded by Matthew and Mark?

The first of these questions is the harder to answer, as there is such a delightful difference of opinion among commentators and critics on this point. Many hold that the high-priest was no other than Annas, and that after this preliminary examination before him Jesus was led away to Caiaphas, before whom the real trial took place. So Meyer, Wieseler, Lange, Neander, Ellicott, Alford, Godet. Others are equally positive that we have no record of the proceedings before Annas, and that the preliminary examination was conducted by Caiaphas, the high-priest. So De Wette, Tholuck, Lücke, Friedlieb, Gresswell, Robinson, Gardiner. When so many and so learned doctors disagree, there seems to be no way for those of humbler pretensions but to examine the evidence on both sides, and to decide, with becoming modesty, each for himself.

The decision of this mooted point depends mainly upon the interpretation of two passages. The first of these is John xviii. 19: ‘Ο οὖν ἀρχιερεὺς ἠρώτησε τὸν Ἰησοῦν περὶ τῶν μαθητῶν αὐτοῦ καὶ περὶ τῆς διδαχῆς αὐτοῦ. The other is John xviii. 24: Ἀπέστειλεν οὖν αὐτὸν ὁ Ἄννας δεδεμένον πρὸς Καιάφαν τὸν ἀρχιερέα. Now whom does John call ὁ ἀρχιερεύς, Annas or Caiaphas? The following reasons have been given for supposing that Annas is meant: First, that term is applied to Annas both before and after this (Luke iii. 2; Acts iv. 6). But this is hardly conclusive; for the question is as to John's usage of the term.[1] Secondly, John calls Caiaphas ἀρχιερεὺς τοῦ ἐνιαυτοῦ ἐκείνου (xviii. 13).

[1] See Alford and Meyer, in loco. Compare also Andrews, Life of Our Lord, p. 486.

Neander[1] considers this proof that John intends to make a distinction between Annas, the high-priest *de jure*, and Caiaphas, the high-priest *de facto*. On the other hand, it is certain that John nowhere calls Annas the high-priest, unless here. And we can hardly suppose that he applies that title to Annas here; for in the second of the two passages above quoted he expressly calls Caiaphas the high-priest, without any qualification whatsoever. The usage of Matthew is the same (xxvi. 57). We conclude, then, that the natural interpretation of John's language is clearly in favor of the supposition that the ἀρχιερεύς in question was Caiaphas, and not Annas. This conclusion is rendered only less than certain by the second of the two passages cited, which is rendered in the King James version, "Now Annas had sent him bound unto Caiaphas, the high-priest." The particle οὖν is wanting in the Textus Receptus; consequently, many have held that ἀπέστειλεν should be translated as a simple aorist, "Annas *sent* him bound," etc. This would make it necessary to regard the preliminary examination as having taken place before Annas. But, though many have held this opinion, few hold it now; for ἀπέστειλεν οὖν αὐτόν κ.τ.λ. is unquestionably the true reading. It has the support of ℵ, B, C (*pr. man.*), L, X, Δ, the Syriac and Ethiopic versions, and is adopted by Tischendorf, Tregelles, and Alford. Moreover, the use of the aorist as a pluperfect is not infrequent.[2] Compare with the use of ἀπέστειλεν, ἔδησεν and ἔθετο in Matt. xiv. 3; and of ἔδωκεν, xxvi. 48; of ὑπήντησεν, in John xi. 30; and of ἡτοίμασαν, in Luke xxiv. 1. Another corroborative circumstance is found in the following consideration: If the examination took place before Caiaphas, then Peter's denial also occurred there. This does away with the clumsy and improbable hypothesis that Annas and Caiaphas occupied different apartments in the same palace — a hypothesis to which those have been driven who hold the opposite view.

---

[1] Life of Christ (Am. ed.), p. 410, note.

[2] Vid. Winer, Grammar of N. T. Greek, p. 275, and Buttmann, p. 200. In classical Greek, vid. Thucyd. i. 102; Xen. Anab. i. 2. 24; Demos. (Reiske's ed.), 576. 18; ristoph. Nub. 238. Cf. also Crosby's Greek Grammar, § 580.

There is something ludicrous in the statement, "Now Annas sent him away bound to Caiaphas," if the sending away consisted in a removal from one apartment to another in the same house.

We have now to answer the second question — Does Luke describe the same trial as that recorded by Matthew and Mark? It seems clear, from the statements of Matthew and Mark, that there were two sessions of the Sanhedrim — one during the night, and the other early in the morning. The preliminary examination before Caiaphas took place while the Sanhedrim was assembling.[1] When it had assembled a formal examination or trial was instituted, which Matthew and Mark describe at considerable length. At daylight the Sanhedrim reassembled, and after a brief examination Jesus was formally condemned. This scene is probably the one described by Luke, and is barely hinted at by Matthew. The similarity between Luke's account of the morning session and the descriptions that Matthew and Mark give of the night session has led many to suppose that there was really but one session. It is to be borne in mind, however, that Matthew and Mark state that at the night session the Jews attempted to find testimony against Jesus, and failed miserably. He was finally condemned out of his own mouth. When they reassembled in the morning to pass formal sentence upon Jesus, what could be more natural than that they should again ask him the fatal question, and that he should repeat substantially his former answer?

The most probable order of events, then, is as follows: Jesus is led to Annas, who sends him bound to Caiaphas; while the Sanhedrim is assembling Caiaphas examines Jesus; the Sanhedrim having assembled, Jesus is tried and condemned; a recess is taken, during which Jesus is abused by

[1] Cf. Matt. xxvi. 57 and Mark xiv. 53. Matthew says that the Sanhedrim *assembled* (συνήχθησαν), and proceeds at once to the formal trial. Mark says, with his usual accuracy, the Sanhedrim *are assembling* (συνέρχονται) when Jesus is brought to Caiaphas. It should seem, then, that this examination took place while the Sanhedrim was assembling, and so soon as a *quorum* got together the trial proceeded.

the rabble; in the morning the Sanhedrim reassembles, reexamines Jesus, passes formal sentence upon him, and leads him away to Pilate. The trial before the Roman governor presents no chronological difficulties of importance, and need therefore claim none of our attention at present.

Dissertation II. — Legal Aspects of the Trial.

The trial and execution of a man is a most awful scene. In it men solemnly discharge the most solemn trust committed to governments by God. It is obvious that so weighty a matter should be conducted decently and in order. No haste should deprive the accused of a fair opportunity of defence. No passion or prejudice should sway judge or jury, and so prevent an impartial verdict. The guilt of the accused should be clearly proved by trustworthy witnesses, and if a reasonable doubt of his guilt remain justice should be tempered with mercy. This is the ideal trial, of which the reality may indeed always fall short, but which every trial should as nearly as possible realize. This ideal is clearly recognized in the Jewish criminal procedure, as laid down in the law and supplemented in the Talmud, and as expounded by the ablest Jewish writers, both ancient and modern. Salvador, a Jewish writer, in his Histoire des Institutions de Moïse et du peuple Hébreu, gives two admirable chapters on the penal code of the Jews. According to him, there were four rules which were fundamental in Jewish criminal jurisprudence: (1) strictness in the accusation; (2) publicity in the discussion; (3) full freedom granted to the accused; (4) assurance against all dangers of errors of testimony.[1] In later times so completely was the accused hedged about by legal safeguards, that conviction in capital cases became almost impossible, and the saying arose that "the Sanhedrim which condemns a man to death, even once in seven years, is a slaughter-house."[2] A trial conducted according to the spirit of these rules could not fail of being a fair one.

But this was not all. Specific and minute rules were laid

---

[1] I. 365.   [2] Mishna, Treatise Makhoth.

down for the conduct of the trial. These were afterwards embodied in the Mishna; and the passage, as quoted by Surenhusius, is so significant that it is subjoined nearly in full:

"Money trials and trials for life have the same rules of inquiry and investigation. But they differ in procedure in the following points: The former require only three, the latter three and twenty, judges. In the former, it matters not on which side the judges speak who give the first opinions; in the latter, those who are in favor of acquittal must speak first. In the former, a majority of one is always enough; in the latter, a majority of one is enough to acquit, but it requires a majority of two to condemn. In the former, a decision may be quashed on review (for error), no matter which way it has gone; in the latter, a condemnation may be quashed, but not an acquittal. In the former, disciples of the law present in the court may speak (as assessors) on either side; in the latter, they may speak in favor of the accused, but not against him. In the former, a judge who has indicated his opinion, no matter on which side, may change his mind; in the latter, he who has given his voice for guilt may change his mind, but not he who has given his voice for acquittal. The former (money trials) are commenced only in the daytime, but may be concluded after nightfall; the latter (capital trials) are commenced only in the daytime, and must also be concluded during the day. The former may be concluded by acquittal or condemnation on the day on which they have begun; the latter may be concluded on that day if there is a sentence of acquittal, but must be postponed to a second day if there is to be a condemnation. And for this reason capital trials are not held on the day before a Sabbath or a feast-day." [1]

"If a man is found innocent, the court absolves him. But if not, his judgment is put off to the following day. Meantime the judges meet together, and, eating little meat and drinking no wine during that whole day, they confer upon the cause. On the following morning they return into court

[1] Mishna, De Synedriis, iv. 1.

[and vote over again, with the like precautions as before].
..... If judgment is at last pronounced, they bring out the man sentenced to stone him. The place of punishment is to be apart from the place of judgment (for it is said in Lev. xxiv. 14, 'Bring the blasphemer without the camp'). In the meantime an officer is to stand at the door of the court with a handkerchief in his hand; another, mounted on horseback, follows the procession so far, but halts at the farthest point where he can see the man with the handkerchief. [The judges remain sitting], and if any one offers himself to prove that the condemned man is innocent he at the door waves the handkerchief, and the horseman instantly gallops after the condemned, and recalls him for his defence."[1]

Most of these principles, as is admitted by modern Jewish writers, were as firmly established in Christ's day as when they were finally committed to writing in the Mishna. It only remains to inquire how far these principles were observed in the trial of Jesus. And it will not be amiss to consider, by way of preliminary, whether the Sanhedrim was in a frame of mind that made a fair trial a possibility. From an examination of the facts at our command, only one conclusion can be drawn. Early in the second year of Christ's ministry the Jews sought to kill him, and similar attempts were frequently made during the rest of his life (John v. 16; cf. vii. 1, 19, 20; viii. 40, 59; x. 31). John, especially, is very explicit on this point. The terrific denunciations which Jesus had launched at the hypocrisy of the pharisees had aroused their unbounded wrath. Their hatred had burned fiercer and fiercer, until, after the raising of Lazarus, they resolved to put him to death (John xi. 47–54). But Jesus was exceedingly popular. His teachings had taken deep hold upon the people (Luke viii. 40; Mark xii. 37; John xi. 48; xii. 19). Unless he could be rendered odious in the eyes of the multitude, the rulers well knew that any attempt against him would recoil upon their own heads. They accordingly sought pretexts against him in various ways.

[1] Mishna, De Synedriis, v. 5 and vi. 1.

They endeavored to embroil him with the Roman government by asking him if it were lawful to pay tribute to Caesar. Note the craft implied in Matthew's description of the scene: "Then went the pharisees, and took counsel how they might entangle him in his talk" (xxii. 15). Luke is even more explicit: "And they watched him, and sent forth spies (καθέτους), which should feign themselves just men, that they might take hold of his words, that so they might deliver him unto the power and authority of the governor" (xx. 20). Finally, during the passover they assembled and "consulted that they might take Jesus by subtlety (δόλῳ, *by fraud*), and kill him. But they said, Not on the feast-day (μὴ ἐν τῇ ἑορτῇ) lest there be an uproar among the people" (Matt. xxvi. 4, 5). When Judas offered to betray his master, this objection was done away with. If the rulers could seize Jesus secretly, and try and condemn him upon some charge or other before the people could know what was going on, the ever fickle rabble might be persuaded to acquiesce in their action. So, at least thought the Sanhedrim, and the sequel proved the plan well laid. It is evident, then, that the Sanhedrim was not at all disposed to grant Jesus a fair trial. The case was prejudged. The verdict was already determined. The rulers had resolved to destroy Jesus, and the trial was but a trial for appearances' sake. The whole scene was a solemn farce.

An examination of the trial would be incomplete without a glance at the arrest of Jesus; for this arrest has a most significant bearing upon the after proceedings. The arrest was marked by secrecy and stealth. Midnight was selected as the most favorable time. This does not of itself prove the arrest to be illegal, because a legal arrest might have been made at night for the sake of avoiding an uproar among the people. But the *posse comitatus* was a mere mob (ὄχλος, Mark xiv. 43), armed with swords and clubs (ξύλων, Mark xiv. 43) which they had hastily snatched as they rushed along. To be sure, John says that Judas was attended by the band and officers, and this would seem to imply some sort of order, as "the band" undoubtedly refers to the band of Levites who formed the guard of the temple.[1] The leader of the band John calls χιλίαρχος, *captain*. With this band came also the ὑπηρέται, or *officers*,[2] who were to make the arrest. But along with these — or rather, mingled with these — came a disorderly rabble, composed of the loungers about the temple and the "roughs" of Jerusalem. So little did the whole affair look like a legal proceeding, so much did it look like mob-law, that the disciples prepared to resist those who attempted to arrest Jesus. This they would hardly have ventured to do had the arrest been regular and legal. This view is still further confirmed by the fact that Peter was not arrested for his resistance to the officers, nor molested when afterwards recognized in the palace of the high-priest.

The Preliminary Examinations.

As only John mentions the examination before Annas, — and even he barely mentions it, — we may pass it by with the remark that such an examination was extra-judicial, if not illegal. Annas, we are informed by Josephus,[3] had been

---

[1] Many commentators have supposed that the phrase λαβὼν τὴν σπεῖραν is to be referred to a cohort of Roman soldiers, but there is no evidence in favor of such an opinion. To be sure σπεῖρα is everywhere else in the New Testament used to designate a Roman cohort, but in each case the word is qualified by the addition of some distinctive term (cf. Acts x. 1; xxi. 31; xxvii. 1). Of itself, the word is indefinite, meaning any band of armed men. Josephus uses σπεῖρα to designate the Levitical temple guard, which is referred to in the following Old Testament passages: Ps. cxxxiv. 1; 2 Kings xii. 9; xxv. 18; 1 Chron. ix. 17, 27 sq.; 2 Chron. xxxv. 8. The term σπεῖρα is applied to this guard in the Apocrypha: Judith xiv. 11; 2 Mac. viii. 23. As for the terms χιλίαρχος and στρατηγός nothing could be plainer than that they are not used in a strict military sense. Josephus frequently uses them to designate the officers of the temple guard. Vid. Bell. Jud., ii. 12, 16; vi. 5. 3; Antiq. xx. 6. 2; cf. 1 Esdras i. 9 and 2 Mac. iii. 4, where apparently the same officer is called προστάτης τοῦ ἱεροῦ. If the band had been Roman soldiers the Sanhedrim must have applied to Pilate for them. This would have necessitated charges against Jesus. That the Sanhedrim had made no such application and brought no such charges is amply proved by Pilate's question on the following morning, "What accusation bring ye against this man?" He knew of no charge against Jesus up to that time. If, then, there were any Roman soldiers present — as is by no means unlikely — they belonged not to the σπεῖρα but to the ὄχλος.

[2] The ὑπηρέται seem to have corresponded closely in their functions to the Roman *lictors*.

[3] Antiq., xviii. 2. 2.

deposed from the priesthood some time previously, and had therefore no jurisdiction in the case.

To one accustomed to the methods of modern criminal jurisprudence there would seem to be nothing illegal in an examination by Caiaphas, the *de facto* high-priest. In France, in England, or in our own country, for example, an accused person on his arrest is taken before a magistrate, and an examination follows. If sufficient evidence is produced to render his guilt probable, he is committed for trial by the magistrate, or admitted to bail, if the nature of the offence permits it. If, on the contrary, the evidence is frivolous, or the prisoner's innocence probable, he is discharged at once. But in the Jewish law this was not the procedure. It was the right of the accused to be free from all investigation until he was brought to trial before the Sanhedrim. This is considered by Salvador one of the strong points of Hebrew law. He says: "The accused man is not submitted to secret examinations, in which through his trouble the innocent might furnish deadly weapons against himself."[1] It goes without saying, however, that if Jesus was to be subjected to an illegal examination, the high-priest was bound to see that it was fairly conducted. Caiaphas does nothing of the kind. He calls for no witnesses, but begins to question Jesus about his disciples and doctrine, hoping thus to find some pretext for an accusation. This well-laid plan is overturned by the straightforward, almost brusque, answer: "I have spoken openly to the world; I ever taught in the synagogue and in the temple whither all the Jews resort; and in secret have I said nothing. Why askest thou me? Ask them who heard me what I have said unto them; behold, they know what I said." In these words Jesus demanded, as was his right, that the accusations against him should be made good by competent witnesses. He declined to give evidence against himself. Irritated by this bold reply and its implied rebuke, one of the bystanders — an officer of the Sanhedrim, John says (xviii. 22) — smote Jesus in the face.

[1] i. 366.

This indignity was in clear defiance not only of the spirit, but of the letter, of Jewish law. On a similar occasion the high-priest commanded Paul to be smitten, when the apostle's fierce wrath flamed forth in a scathing denunciation: " God shall smite thee, thou whited wall: for sittest thou to judge me after the law, and commandest me to be smitten contrary to the law?" It may be pleaded that this was the act of a single individual, for which neither the Sanhedrim nor the high-priest can be held responsible. But was the officer who had so offended the majesty of the law by smiting an uncondemned person rebuked by high-priest or Sanhedrim? Their very silence approved the act. Let the reader picture to himself, if he can, a similar case in one of our own courts — the sheriff smiting the prisoner at the bar, and the court looking on in complacent and approving silence!

The Trial before the Sanhedrim.

The *time* of the trial was illegal. No point is more certain with reference to Jewish laws than that trials by night were strictly prohibited. The passages already quoted from the Mishna are quite sufficient to establish this point, and there are numerous others. Lightfoot quotes the following passage from the Talmud : " Judicia capitalia transigunt interdiu, et finiunt interdiu."[1] A gloss on this passage says : " Ne judicent vesperiis Sabbati, nec vesperiis dici festi." Schöttgen quotes the following : " Sessiones judicii instituendae sunt in mane."[2] With these statements all Jewish writers who have treated of this subject agree.[3] Maimonides says : " Judicia neque noctu, neque sabbato, peragere licitum erat — non inchoant judicia noctu."[4]

Again, the *place* of the trial is illegal. This night session of the Sanhedrim was held in the palace of Caiaphas. Of this fact the evangelists leave us in no doubt. But Jewish tradi-

---

[1] Gem. Babyl. Sanhedr. iv. 1, vid. Hor. Heb. in Matt. xxvii. 1.
[2] Hor. Heb. in John xviii. 28.
[3] Cf. Salvador, Livre iv. chapitre 2, Administration de la Justice, passim.
[4] Vide Gresswell's Dissertations, Vol. iii. p. 205.

tion, with one voice, affirms that no trial was legal, and no sentence valid, unless the trial was held and the sentence pronounced in the gazzith (גָּזִית), or council-chamber, in the temple. So firmly was this custom established that it had all the force of a law, and "to migrate from the gazzith" is synonymous with losing the power of capital punishment. Thus Lightfoot quotes from the Talmud: "Quadraginta annis ante excidium Templi, migravit Synedrium, et sedit in Tabernis."[1] A gloss in this passage says: "Cum ergo non sederunt in conclavi gazzith, non judicarunt de iis [poenis] et sic cessarunt judicia ista mulctativa." Another gloss is substantially the same: "Non judicarunt de capitalibus in Synedriis inferioribus in aliqua civitate, nisi dum sederet Synedrium magnum in conclavi gazzith."

The *conduct* of the trial was grossly illegal. The Sanhedrim sought long and diligently for evidence, but found themselves unable to substantiate any valid charge against Jesus. Witnesses could be obtained in abundance, — witnesses only too ready to accuse the prisoner of more than one crime, — but, unfortunately, their testimony did not agree. Finally, there came forward two who testified that they heard Jesus say: "I will destroy this temple that is made with hands, and within three days I will build another that is made without hands." Yet even in this, as Mark significantly adds, the testimony did not agree. The evidence of the suborned witnesses was worthless. The plot of the pharisees proved an utter failure. So when the highpriest exclaimed, "Answerest thou nothing?" Jesus remained silent. There was no need of an answer; the confused and contradictory testimony confuted itself. Thereupon Caiaphas, enraged at the failure of the plot, fearful that Jesus might after all escape for want of evidence against him, as a last

[1] Abodah Zarah, viii. 2; Hor. Heb. in John xviii. 31. This passage is quoted here merely to illustrate a verbal usage. No opinion is intended to be expressed as to the accuracy of the historical statement. In point of fact, the statement is believed to be untrustworthy, and the reasons for this belief are given below in the third Dissertation.

resort administers the Sanhedrim oath[1]: "*I adjure thee by the living God* that thou tell us if thou be the Christ, the Son of God." Here is a flagrant violation of a fundamental maxim of all criminal jurisprudence. All civilized codes, at least, agree that a man is to be held innocent until he is proved guilty. No code of laws permits a judge to place the accused under oath in order to compel him to give testimony against himself. Jewish law and Jewish tradition are alike clear on this point. Two trustworthy witnesses, at least, were required for conviction — "At the mouth of two witnesses shall he that is worthy of death be put to death; but at the mouth of one witness he shall not be put to death," wrote the great lawgiver of Israel (Deut. xvii. 6). "One witness is no witness," says the Talmud; and Salvador distinctly says: "Our law never condemns on the simple avowal of the accused." But the high-priest had resolved that, on one pretext or another, Jesus should be put to death. Justice had no place in his plans. Caiaphas has forced Jesus to do one of two things. He must answer in the affirmative, and criminate himself, or he must answer in the negative, and publicly renounce his Messianic claims. In the one case, the Sanhedrim will have a pretext for putting him to death; in the other, the Jewish hierarchy need fear no longer the pseudo-Messiah. To the adjuration Jesus responded: "Thou hast said" — a Hebraistic form of emphatic affirmation. He well knew that these words, in which he proclaimed his Messiahship and divinity, would be his death-sentence; nevertheless, the Everlasting sware by himself that he was the promised one who should redeem his people. For this, the watchword of redemption, Israel had longed and waited for many weary centuries; now it is heard only to be repudiated. That declaration to which saints and patriarchs had

---

[1] It is universally admitted that this was the usual form of administering that oath. By the simple yea or nay the witness took the oath upon himself, and swore by the living God that his testimony was true. Grotius says (in loco): ἐξορκίζειν, Hebraice השביע, modo est jurejurando adigere, interdum verum obscurare. With this compare Michaelis, Laws of Moses, § 302, and Selden's chapter De Juramentis, in his book on Sanhedrims.

looked forward with yearnings unspeakable is reckoned a crime worthy of death. For, when the high-priest heard the answer, he rent his clothes in simulated horror, exclaiming: "He hath spoken blasphemy! What further need have we of witnesses? Behold, ye have heard the blasphemy. What think ye?" And the entire Sanhedrim shouted, with one voice, "He is אִישׁ מָוֶת (a man of death)."

The mockery and insults which ensued are so manifestly illegal, and so disgraceful withal, that Salvador says of them: "As to the ill-treatment which followed the sentence, *it was contrary to the spirit of the Jewish law;* and it is not in the course of nature that a senate composed of the most respectable men of a nation, who, however they might have been deceived, yet intended to act legally, should have permitted *such outrages* against him whose life was at their disposal. The writers who have transmitted to us these details, not having been present at the trial, have been disposed to exaggerate the picture, either on account of their prejudices or to throw greater obloquy on the judges."[1] It is enough for our present purpose that these acts are acknowledged to have been outrages, and are conceded to be illegal. It is not in our province to contend for the credibility of the Gospels; that is taken for granted.

We come now to the morning session. The Jewish law ordained that final sentence should not be passed upon a criminal on the same day with the trial. This wise provision was made, no doubt, in order that, if a trial had been held in haste or in the heat of passion, the Sanhedrim might have an opportunity to reconsider, and, if advisable, to reverse their first decision. This provision is laid down in the most explicit terms by the Talmud, and is recognized repeatedly in the works of Jewish writers on jurisprudence. "Judicia de capitalibus finiunt eodem die, si sint ad absolutionem; si vero sint ad damnationem, finiuntur die sequente," is one of the maxims of the Talmud.[2] A favorite saying among the

---

[1] Cf. Institutions du Moïse, etc. Livre, iv. ch. 3, passim.
[2] Moed. Katon., v. 1. Lightfoot, ubi supra.

rabbins was: "Beatus est judex qui fermentat judicium suum"; and a gloss explains this as meaning "qui judicium moratur, et pernoctare facit, ut ventilet veritatem." Salvador even says that the judges were to postpone sentence until the third day. Notwithstanding their fiery haste, the Jews seemed to feel that some little show of complying with the legal forms was needful, and accordingly in the morning they led Jesus away into the council-chamber[1] to ratify their previous action. But this was only an evasion of the law. The Jewish day is reckoned from sunset to sunset. Therefore the trial held in the night and the sentence passed in the morning fell within the same day. This morning session, like everything else connected with the trial, was a farce — a pretence only of conforming to legal procedure. It is quite possible that the Sanhedrim would have dispensed altogether with the second session had not more summary proceedings been out of the question. It was impossible for them to take Jesus before Pilate until morning;[2] and this fact may have caused the delay, more than any lingering respect for legal forms. They "e'en made a virtue of necessity," as many other folk have been compelled to do.

As to the trial before Pilate, there needs no proof that sentence was finally pronounced without the slightest evidence of guilt, in clear violation alike of law and of justice, since Pilate himself said as much again and again.

Dissertation III. — The Jewish Autonomy.

The trial of Jesus by Pilate gives rise to a question re-

[1] It has been generally supposed that the scene of the trial was not changed — that after the night trial was over Jesus was removed from the hall and mocked, and in the morning was led back (ἀνήγαγον) into the hall, where the Sanhedrim had reassembled. But Tischendorf, Tregelles, and Alford read not ἀνήγαγον (T. R.), but ἀπήγαγον, following ℵ, B, D, K, T, etc. The ἀπό would seem to indicate that Jesus was led *away* to some little distance. It is most probable, therefore, that this morning session was held in the gazzith, or council-chamber of the temple. Cf. Gresswell's Dissertations, Vol. iii. p. 204.

[2] Sepp quotes (Leben Jesu, Vol. iii. p. 484), from Roman writers to prove that, according to Roman law, a night trial was illegal. Macrobius says: Magistratus post meridiam noctem auspicantur et post exortum solem agunt. Senatus consulta ante exortum solem aut post solis occasum facta, rata non esse. — Saturn. i. 3.

garding the Jewish autonomy after the Roman conquest. Did the Sanhedrim have jurisdiction over capital offences against Jewish law? With rare exceptions, commentators and historians have answered this question in the negative. At the very least, they have held that the jurisdiction of the Sanhedrim was only nominal — that the form of trial and condemnation might be gone through, but that sentence of death could not be executed without the Roman procurator's approval. It may therefore seem presumptuous to call in question so time-honored a conclusion; and yet, in this sceptical age, the mere antiquity of a theory goes for little. A new survey of the evidence for and against this particular theory can at any rate do no harm, and may lead us to clearer conceptions of the relations between the Jewish nation and their Roman conquerors. Let us first, then, examine the grounds for the opinion that at the time of Christ's trial the Jews had lost their autonomy, at least so far as the *jus gladii* is concerned.

Josephus relates the following incident: After the death of Festus, Albinus was appointed procurator of Judea by Nero. Before his arrival Ananus, the high-priest, — whom Josephus describes as "a bold man in his temper and very insolent," — convened the Sanhedrim, and brought before that body James the brother of Christ and others, who were condemned to death, and stoned. When Albinus arrived he caused Ananus to be deposed from the priesthood, on the ground, as Josephus states, "that it was not lawful for Ananus to assemble a Sanhedrim without his [the procurator's] consent."[1] This is often quoted as settling the whole question. But observe, Josephus says nothing explicitly about the power of life and death, and this very silence furnishes a presumption that the Jews had not lost their autonomy. The misdemeanor of the high-priest was not that he put to death a criminal without the procurator's sanction, but that he assembled the Sanhedrim without such sanction. This is not a distinction without a difference; for Selden considers

[1] Antiq., xx. 9. 1.

it probable that the procurator in the beginning of his rule sanctioned the assembling of the Sanhedrim once for all, and formally empowered it to try and punish all offenders against its own laws.[1] At all events, this incident is no very strong evidence for the theory that we are considering.

The Talmud is held to furnish more conclusive testimony on this point. Selden quotes from the Jerusalem Gemara: "Traditio. Quadraginta annis ante vastatum Templum, ablata sunt judicia capitalia ab Israele."[2] At best, this statement is only a vague tradition, which was not committed to writing for several centuries after the event it professes to record. But the Talmud is not even consistent on this point; for another passage, quoted by the same author, states that during this period the Jews employed no less than four distinct methods of capital punishment.[3] But grant that the statement is strictly true. The temple was destroyed in August 823 A.U.C. Forty years before was 783 A.U.C. Very many of the best chronological authorities adopt this as the year of Christ's death (so Wieseler, Friedlieb, Gresswell, Ellicott, Thomson, Andrews). This leaves a very narrow margin; for, in the absence of all records, who shall say whether it was earlier or later in that year than the Passover that the *jus gladii* was taken from the Jews? Besides, many eminent chronologists — for example, Browne, Sepp. Patritius — adopt the year 782 A.U.C. as the true date of Christ's death. If this be the correct date — and who shall say that it is not, when the whole subject is in so much doubt? — there is a whole year against the theory in question. In short, the passage from the Talmud is utterly worthless as evidence on this point. Selden, who is perhaps the highest single authority on the subject, concludes that we can only infer from the Talmud that during this period the procurator may sometimes have

---

[1] Selden, De Synedriis et Præfecturis Juridicis Veterum Ebraeorum (London, 1726), lib. ii. c. 15. 11.

[2] Lightfoot, Hor. Heb., in Matt. xxvi. 3 and John xviii. 31.

[3] Selden, ubi supra. — Quod magis est dicendum de quadriginta illis excidium anteverterunt annis, quibus etiam quatuor poenae capitales in usu. Non penitus sublata sunt seu non prorsus desiere. Et again: A die quo excisum est Templum, quamvis cessarit Synedrium, tamen non cessarunt quatuor mortes.

interfered with the Jewish autonomy. Friedlieb goes still farther, and decisively pronounces the statement of the Talmud incorrect, because Judea became a Roman province sixty years before the destruction of Jerusalem, and the Jewish autonomy was lost then, if ever.

The analogy of the Roman law is pleaded. M. Dupin quotes at some length from Roman law-writers to prove that the power of life and death " was a principal attribute of sovereignty, which the Romans always took great care to reserve to themselves, even if they neglected other things." [1] Tacitus speaks to the same effect: " Apud Romanos jus valet gladii; cetera transmittuntur." [2] Certainly M. Dupin makes out a strong case, but it is by no means without a flaw. We learn from Strabo that Marseilles did not lose its autonomy, and from the same authority we know that the Syrians lost the *jus gladii* only under the reign of Claudius, and then as a punishment for having put Roman citizens to death. Roman practice in this regard was not uniform; yet there is no doubt that the usual custom was as M. Dupin states. Hence the analogy furnishes a strong presumption — but, after all, only a presumption — that the power of life and death was lost to the Jews when first conquered.

The *locus classicus* of the theory we are considering is John xviii. 31: " Then said Pilate unto them, Take ye him and judge him according to your law.[3] The Jews therefore said unto him, It is not lawful for us ($\dot{\eta}\mu\hat{\iota}\nu$ $o\dot{\upsilon}\kappa$ $\ddot{\epsilon}\xi\epsilon\sigma\tau\iota\nu$) to put any man to death." This is generally quoted with a triumphant air which implies that there is nothing further to be said. But are these words so conclusive as they are often

[1] Jésus devant Pilate, pp. 55-62. M. Dupin's principal authorities are Loiseau-Godefroy and Cujas.

[2] Ann. xv. 31.

[3] It seems hardly necessary to remark that these words ill accord with the theory that the Jews had not the *jus gladii*. Pilate takes for granted their power to punish Jesus. Still less in accordance with the theory are his words a little further on : " Take ye him and crucify him, for I find no fault in him " (John xix. 6). It has, indeed, been said that Pilate spoke these words mockingly; but the Jewish mob was hardly in a humor for Pilate to venture a sneer at their demands.

considered? Although the Jews had passed sentence of death upon Jesus, they dared not execute the sentence. "They feared the people." But a day or two before Jesus had entered Jerusalem amid the acclamations of thousands. His teachings in the temple during the passover week had made a profound impression. His adherents were both numerous and powerful, and the Sanhedrim dared not risk a collision with them. Moreover, Jewish law forbade the execution of a criminal during the feast.[1] To be sure, the Sanhedrim had already shown how little the rulers of the nation were bound by their own traditions and laws; but there were lengths to which they dared not go. To condemn Jesus upon a false charge of blasphemy, and so prejudice many against him, was one thing; to execute him during the most solemn feast of the nation, and draw down on their own heads the charge of sacrilege, was quite another. But, on the other hand, the Sanhedrim had strong reasons for wishing Jesus to be put to death without delay. If this pretended Messiah could be executed before the eyes of his followers, it would strike terror into them, and be the death-blow of this new heresy. So they fondly thought. Accordingly, they take him before Pilate, and prefer a charge of sedition. But Pilate finds in him no fault at all, and says, "Take ye him, and judge him according to your law." It was plain enough to the astute Roman that if Jesus was guilty of any offence at all it was against Jewish law, and so an offence which as a Roman procurator he had neither the right nor the disposition to judge. But the Jewish rulers, seeing their last chance slip from them, cry out, "It is not lawful for us to put any man to death" — for a political offence; and they press again the charge of sedition.[2] That this is the natural meaning of these words is proved by the whole context.

---

[1] Says the Talmud: Non judicant die festo. Lightfoot, ubi supra.

[2] There is no ground for the usual assertion that the Jews prepared a double charge against Jesus when they brought him before Pilate. Not one of the Evangelists mentions any charge but that of sedition. That was the only charge over which Pilate had jurisdiction, and it was the one offence over which the Jews, from the nature of the case, could have no jurisdiction. Had the Jews

To sum up: We find in favor of this theory only a strong presumption, supported by evidence more or less unsatisfactory and inconclusive. Still, the presumption is so strong, and the evidence as a whole so weighty, that, unless some positive evidence against it is forthcoming, the theory must stand. Let us now examine the opposite theory, that the Jews at this time possessed the *jus gladii* in capital offences against their own laws.

Certain passages are cited from Josephus which seem inconsistent with any other theory. On one occasion, we are told, Herod was summoned before the Sanhedrim to answer for having executed a Jew without the approval of that body.[1] But if the Sanhedrim had not the right to execute the sentence of the law, surely they had no right to call any one to account for so doing. After the death of Herod, we find in Josephus no intimation that the Jews were deprived of the power which they evidently possessed during his reign. He does inform us, however, that the Jews desired to be joined to the province of Syria, and to be governed by a procurator, because they hoped for greater freedom under the Roman rule than under that of Herod's tyrannical sons.[2] Their wish was granted. Had they been disappointed in their hope, — in other words, had they been deprived of their autonomy, — it is inconceivable that Josephus should not have recorded the fact. Again, we are expressly told that the Jews did possess the power of life and death in certain cases. Gentiles who entered the inner court of the temple were put to death.[3] The Essenes adopted a Draconian code, and punished every offence against the law of Moses with death.[4] The Sadducees were "very rigid in judging all offenders, above all the rest of the Jews."[5]

stated that Jesus was condemned on the charge of blasphemy, and requested Pilate's approval of the sentence, then we might infer that the Jews no longer possessed the *jus gladii*. But instead they prefer a wholly new charge — an offence against Roman, not Jewish law. This is another incidental proof that they possessed the power to execute their sentence, but dared not exercise it.

[1] Antiq., xiv. 19, 3 and 4. [2] Ibid., xvii. 9. 4; cf. 13. 1.
[3] Bell. Jud., vi. 2. 4. [4] Ibid., ii. 8, 9.
[5] Antiq., xx. 9. 1. (cf. Life, § 34).

Various passages in the Gospels strongly confirm this view. In warning his disciples of the persecutions they must undergo, Christ said, "They will deliver you up to councils" (εἰς συνέδρια), i.e. for punishment (Mark xiii. 9). How often, too, are we told that "the Jews sought to kill Jesus" (John v. 18; vii. 1, 25, 26, et al.). This was not mere mob-violence; for on one occasion the Sanhedrim itself in solemn conclave came to the same resolution (John xi. 47–53). When the woman taken in adultery was brought before Jesus, he takes for granted their power to punish her: "*He* that is without sin among you, let him first cast a stone at her."[1]

There are indications in the Acts plainly in favor of the theory that the Jews possessed the *jus gladii* during the lifetime of the apostles. Early in the history of the church at Jerusalem we find the Sanhedrim resolving to slay the disciples of Christ, until dissuaded for a time by Gamaliel (Acts v. 33 sq.); and the martyrdom of Stephen shows that they were not long in carrying their resolution into practice. To be sure, this execution was irregular, but it does not seem to have been illegal, for the procurator took no notice of it. The life of Paul also furnishes several cases just in point. He himself says: "And many of the saints did I shut up in prison, having received authority from the chief priests; and when they were put to death I gave my voice against them" (Acts xxvi. 10). These words can only mean that the saints were put to death by the Sanhedrim, and that Paul as a member of that body voted against them. When Paul was rescued from the Jews in the temple by Lysias the Roman centurion, the latter justified his action in a letter to Felix as follows: "This man was taken of the Jews, and should have been killed of them; then came I with an army and rescued him, having understood that he was a Roman" (Acts xxiii. 27). Now if the Jews had not the power of life and death, their action was illegal in any case, and Lysias was

---

[1] It weakens this argument very little to reply that this passage is of doubtful genuineness. For, granting that the passage is an interpolation, it was interpolated very early, when the historical fact in question must have been well-known, and the interpolator evidently had no idea that the Jews had been deprived of the power to punish this and all other offenses against the Mosaic law.

bound to protect Paul, whether he was a Roman citizen or not. The fact that Paul's Roman citizenship is assigned as the reason for his rescue implies that had he not enjoyed that privilege the Jews would have been left to deal with him according to their own laws. Later, when Festus proposed to give Paul up to the Sanhedrim to be tried by that body, Paul appealed to Caesar (Acts xxv. 11); but wherefore, if the Sanhedrim had neither power to condemn him to death nor to execute the sentence?

While any one of these instances, taken singly, would not suffice to establish the fact that the Jews enjoyed their autonomy at this time, yet taken together they form a chain of proof not easily to be broken. It is one of those points where the evidence is hardly clear enough to warrant a positive decision. Possibly, as Selden thinks,[1] the truth may lie between the two theories. It is not unlikely that the powers of the Sanhedrim and of the procurator were not strictly defined — now one, now the other, may have prevailed, according as the procurator was a firm or a mild ruler. But, at all events, we are warranted in asserting that the time-honored theory that the Jews had utterly lost the *jus gladii* lacks any decisive confirmation.

In studying these closing scenes in the life of our Lord, we have been often reminded of the marvellous fulfilment of the words of the prophet: " He is despised and rejected of men. . . . . . He was oppressed and he was afflicted; yet he opened not his mouth: he is brought as a lamb to the slaughter, and as a sheep before her shearers is dumb, so he opened not his mouth." While studying this trial of Jesus, more than ever before we have realized that we were standing in the presence of one who was more than man. Antiquity lavished praises upon the manly bearing of Socrates during his trial and death. But as we have read and as we have written, not once, nor twice, but many times, has leaped unbidden to our lips that immortal saying of Jean Jacques: " Oui, si la vie et la mort de Socrate sont d'un sage, la vie et la mort de Jésus sont d'un Dieu."

[1] De Synedriis, etc., ubi supra.

ARTICLE

POSITIVISM AS A WORKING SYSTEM.

BY REV. F. H. JOHNSON, ANDOVER, MASS.

"Religion originally spontaneous, then inspired, and afterwards revealed, has at length found its ground in demonstration."—*Auguste Comte.*

"The path of thought, as it were, has taken a sudden turn round a mountain; and our bewildered eyes are staring on an undreamed-of prospect. The leaders of progress thus far have greeted the sight with acclamation, and have confidently declared that we are looking on the promised land. But to the more thoughtful, and to the less impulsive, it is plain that a mist hangs over it, and that we have no right to be sure whether it is the promised land or no. They see grave reasons for making a closer scrutiny, and for asking if, when the mist lifts, what we see will be not splendor but desolation."—*W. H. Mallock.*

A NEW religion is offered to Christendom to take the place of that under which it has been educated. It is offered, and urged upon our acceptance for three reasons:

First, because the Christian religion, as generally received, embodies great errors. It has precious truths wrapped up in superstitions. It presents to the minds of men unreal aims, promises fictitious rewards, frightens them with groundless terrors, appeals to low motives, makes men narrow, egotistical, covetous of personal happiness, is opposed to progress.

Second, because the new religion is a *final* religion, founded upon everlasting truth. It can be *proved* to be true by the nature of things. It makes no demand for faith in the unseen. It appeals to the highest motives only. It presents to man, in the place of an imaginary, personal Deity, a Power that is always here on earth; an ideal which, through all ages, is fitted to inspire his enthusiastic devotion.

Third, because Christendom has outgrown her old religion. It was a religion of provisional and temporary value only. Christianity, as commonly understood, whether true or false,

www.ingramcontent.com/pod-product-compliance
Lightning Source LLC
Chambersburg PA
CBHW031607110426
42742CB00037B/1317